Ludwig van Beethoven

Beethoven at 16

By David Brownell
Illustrated by Nick Taylor

Covers by D. Neary

Front cover: Beethoven, after Tejcek, c. 1824, in front of the Kärntnerthor Theatre, where his glorious concert of May 7 was performed that year; back cover: Beethoven in the *Schwarzspanierhaus* (after Hoechle's sketch) working on the Tenth Symphony.

Chapter One

When Maria and Johann van Beethoven had a son December 16, 1770, the only possible name for him was "Ludwig." Johann's father expected his first grandson to be named after him, and old Ludwig ran the family. He was also Johann's boss.

Old Ludwig had been born a baker's son in Flanders in 1712. He grew up with a fine bass voice, and made a career as a musician—better than getting up in the middle of the night to knead dough. By the time Ludwig was twenty he had been appointed one of the musicians at the court of the Elector of Cologne in Bonn, the city where he spent the rest of his life. He married Maria Josepha Poll, and sold wines as an additional business. Their married life was not happy: she began to drink too much, they separated, and she spent the rest of her days in a local cloister. Ludwig raised their only child, Johann, born in 1739 or 1740, ruling strictly, teaching him music, and taking him into the Elector's service, first as a boy soprano, then as a tenor. In 1761 Ludwig reached the highest rank in his profession by becoming the Elector's *Kapellmeister* (Master of the Chapel)—the leader of the court musicians. His voice was so valued that he continued singing even after his appointment, an unusual thing for a *kapellmeister* to do. He probably composed music for his orchestra to play—most *kapellmeister*s did—but none of it survives.

Ludwig ruled his son as he ruled his orchestra—strictly. But in 1767 Johann rebelled. He wanted to get married. Old Ludwig objected furiously: perhaps he thought Johann was not capable of taking care of a family, perhaps he did not want his tidy household broken up and his control of his son disputed. But for once in his life Johann had his way, and married Maria Magdalena Keverich Laym, the daughter of a superintendent of palace cooks. A widow of twenty-one, whose one child had died, Maria van Beethoven was serious, good-looking, clever, domestic, and delicate in health. Johann gave her his father's place in his life, letting her make the decisions and do the work, but reserving the right to yell at her as loudly as his father had yelled at his mother if a decision turned out badly. Johann brought money home from singing for the court orchestra and from giving music lessons, but the total was not much—he wasn't as good a musician as old Ludwig. When their son was born, they were living in a four-room apartment at the back of a larger house, and the continuing favor of Johann's father was important to their family.

Grandpa Ludwig died when young Ludwig was three: while the boy can't have remembered the old man very well, as he grew up he must have heard many stories from the musicians of the court orchestra about their old *kapellmeister.* Johann did not advance in his profession after his father's death, and it must have been easier for the boy to respect his successful grandfather than his unsuccessful father, whose personal faults were too visible in a small household. All his life Ludwig would refer to "my worthy grandfather," and he kept the old *kapellmeister*'s portrait with him through his many moves.

Johann and Maria had five more children, only two of whom survived to become adults: Carl Caspar, born in 1774, and Nikolaus Johann, born in 1776. (At that period probably half of all children born died during infancy.) The Beethoven family was poor—Johann managed to lose whatever money he had inherited from his father and from Maria's. He hoped to provide a career for his oldest child by teaching him the family trade of music, so that Ludwig too could become a servant of the Elector's.

As young Ludwig grew up, he learned that most of the 10,000 inhabitants of Bonn were servants of the Elector in one way or another. "All of Bonn is fed from the Elector's kitchen," the townspeople said. Their ruler, His Transparency the Archbishop of Cologne, was more important than the size of his little state would suggest: he was one of the handful of Electors of the Holy Roman Empire—the men who elected a new emperor when the old one died. As the ruling Emperor was able to control the selection of new archbishops in the three electorates ruled by churchmen, the Archbishop of Cologne was usually a younger son of the Imperial family, providing at once a good living for one member of a large family and an assurance that the imperial election would be won by the agreed-upon member of the family.

The Archbishop-Elector lived very comfortably in his beautiful little city on the banks of the Rhine. His court was a miniature version of the Imperial Court in Vienna, and His Transparency's servants provided him with the comforts he valued—good food, music, opera, theatre, hunting—whatever he wanted. Good musicians were particularly valued servants in most courts.

Most musicians did work as the servants of rulers, noblemen, or the church at this time: there were no independent orchestras or touring performers, though a few musicians made livings composing or performing in operas. Johann wanted to prepare Ludwig for a job in someone's court. Perhaps, if Ludwig was good enough, he too might become someone's *kapellmeister.*

Johann gave Ludwig his first music lessons—strictly, but not sympathetically. When Ludwig improvised on the piano, Johann rapped his knuckles and told him to keep practicing his exercises. Soon Ludwig was good enough to need a more advanced teacher. Johann hired a drinking companion, Tobias Friedrich Pfeiffer, a tenor and organist. The legend is that Johann and Pfeiffer would come back from the alehouse at midnight and rouse young Ludwig to play for them, punishing the sleepy boy when he made mistakes. Such goings-on would have made the Beethovens unpopular with their neighbors—perhaps neighbors' complaints were one reason for the family habit of moving frequently, a habit that Ludwig kept when he grew up.

It became clear quite soon that Ludwig had real talent, and his father hoped that the boy's talent would bring the family some money right away. If Leopold Mozart had been able to tour around Europe with his children, performing before kings, why not Johann van Beethoven? As a first step, Johann organized a concert for Ludwig in 1778, advertising the boy as being only six, to make sure people would think him a prodigy. But Bonn was too small a town for people to be willing to be impressed by anything a neighbor's brat could do, Johann was not the promoter Leopold Mozart had been, and Ludwig had none of the charm of young Wolfgang Mozart, whom aristocratic ladies had longed to take onto their laps: the concert led no further.

As a boy Beethoven was short, dark, and powerfully, almost clumsily built, with scars from smallpox. Apparently his mother didn't keep the children tidy: people remembered the boy Ludwig as dirty and badly dressed—habits he never outgrew. Between being unattractive and spending most of his time practicing his music, Ludwig had few playmates. He remained in the town's free school until he reached the age limit in 1781. He was a terrible speller, poor at arithmetic, and only fair at foreign languages. His talent was all for music, and he worked at that with all his might, practicing, as he later said, "prodigiously."

In 1782 the new court organist Christian Gottlob Neefe (1748-1798) became Ludwig's teacher, and opened new doors in music and culture for his pupil. Neefe quickly recognized the boy's talent, and let him serve as deputy organist. Ludwig wore the uniform of a court musician, sword and all, and went up to the choir loft on Sundays with his father and the other men of the orchestra. He received no salary, however. By March 1783 Neefe was willing to put in print his opinion that his twelve-year-old pupil "Louis" was "of most promising talent. This youthful genius is deserving of help to enable him to travel. He would surely become a second Wolfgang Amadeus Mozart were he to continue as he has begun." Ten years later, as Ludwig's career began to open up, he wrote gratefully to his old teacher, "I thank you for the counsel which you gave me so often in my progress in my divine art. If I ever become a great man yours shall be a share of the credit."

In 1784 a new Elector came to Bonn—Emperor Joseph II's brother, Archduke Maximilian Franz, a fat, intelligent, gluttonous man who loved

Young Ludwig roused from sleep to play for his father and Pfeiffer

Ludwig, 7½ years old, giving his first concert March 26, 1778, while his father looks on proudly

good music and was one of Mozart's patrons. He was given an inventory of his musical establishment: Johann van Beethoven, (aged 44, "has a very stale voice, has been long in the service, very poor, of fair deportment") was praised less than his son, who worked without a salary, but was rated "of good capability, still young, of good and quiet deportment and poor."

Ludwig's musical talent led him into new places. He read through the scores in the Elector's good musical library, and was hired to teach music to the children of Frau von Breuning, the widow of a state councillor. Many of the intellectual people of Bonn gathered at her home, and Beethoven, who gradually became a friend of the family, even to the point of sleeping there instead of at home, listened to the conversation, read some of the books discussed, and learned about culture, refinement, and new ideas. Eleonore von Breuning, her fiancé Franz Wegeler, and her brothers Lorenz and Stephan became important friends in his development, and their family became his adopted family, calmer, happier, more cultured and comfortable than his own. There Beethoven absorbed the ideas of the Enlightenment philosophers—that all men should work for a world of brotherhood, freedom and tolerance, in which talent would be more important than rank. Neefe helped Beethoven find ways of relating these ideals to his music: a composer should not exist to grind out tunes, but to serve humanity through his art. Beethoven began to think about setting to music the great poet Schiller's "Ode to Joy," which exalts the brotherhood of all men—a project he was not to carry out for many years, but which remained in his mind as part of his youthful ideals.

Teatime at the von Breuning's

Chapter Two

Neefe knew that his pupil had learned all that he could learn in a small town like Bonn, and should travel. A young musician who wanted to learn more about his art had to seek out great musicians in the places where they worked.

As Bonn was a cultural satellite of Vienna, everyone assumed that Beethoven should go there to finish his education. Neefe and Beethoven's other friends hoped that in Vienna Ludwig could become a pupil of the great Mozart. They persuaded someone, probably Elector Maximilian Franz, that his subject had so much talent that he must go to Vienna to cultivate it. The generous patron provided money to pay for the long, expensive journey. Beethoven left Bonn about March 20, 1787, and only arrived in Vienna April 7. He got to see the Emperor, Joseph II, and was introduced to Mozart, who had Beethoven play a piano piece for him, then set him a theme on which to improvise. Beethoven's talent impressed Mozart, who told his friends, "Keep your eye on him; some day he will give the world something to talk about." But Mozart was too busy composing *Don Giovanni* to begin regular lessons with the boy. Still, there would be time for that.

Then, suddenly Beethoven heard from Bonn. His mother was ill—probably dying. He must return. On April 20th, not two weeks after his arrival, he left Vienna. In May he was back in Bonn, watching helplessly as his mother grew weaker. The family were helped in nursing her by their neighbors, the Ries family, several of whose members were also court musicians. Maria van Beethoven died July 17, at the age of forty.

His wife's death seems to have left Johann van Beethoven rudderless. He drank too much, neglecting his family and his work. Someone had to look after him, Ludwig's brothers, who were thirteen and eleven, and their baby sister. Ludwig gave up his dreams of returning to Vienna to take on this burden, but the sense of being trapped in Bonn left him too depressed to do anything. This bad year for the Beethoven family ended with the death of the little daughter at eighteen months.

In the next few years Ludwig earned money playing the organ for the Elector and performing in the orchestra of the Elector's new Bonn National Theatre, where he got to play the operas of many of the best composers of the period. He was composing music himself, as best he could in a household disturbed by his father's irregular habits and two undisciplined adolescent boys. Ludwig was neither old enough nor orderly enough to organize a disorderly household. He struggled with his problems in increasing desperation.

After he had to rescue his father from a policeman who wanted to arrest Johann as a disorderly drunk, Ludwig forced Johann to let Ludwig administer

Beethoven, now 17 and on his first trip to Vienna, plays for a pleased Mozart; 1787

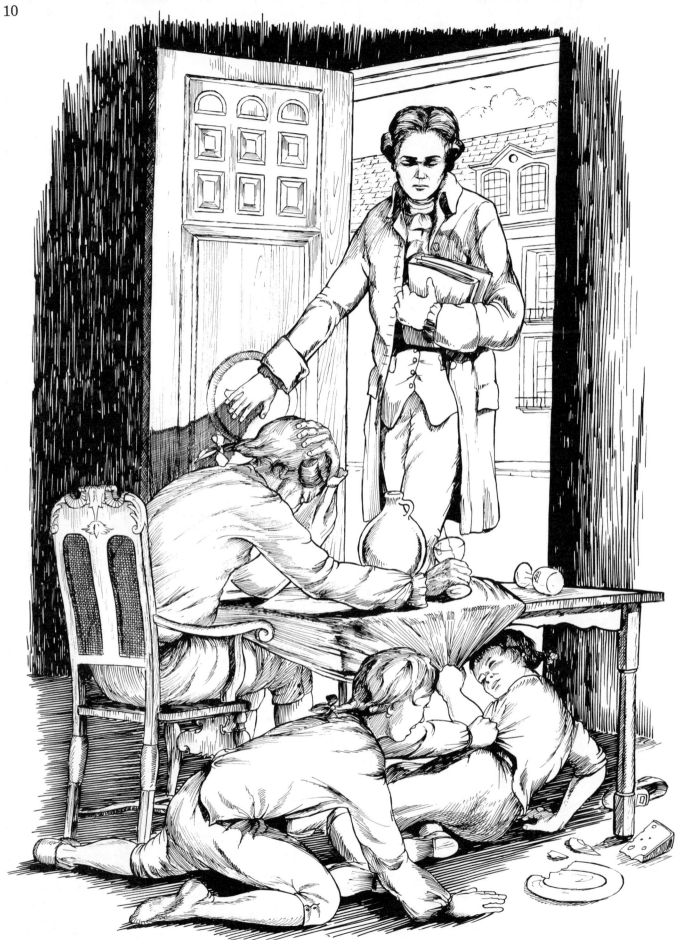

Beethoven returned home to find a drunken father, quarrelling brothers and household squalor, 1787.

his salary. No doubt he felt pity for his father, guilt at having to assume parental authority over him, disgust at his habits, and shame at having them publicly known, as they were in a small town.

Of course not all of Ludwig's life in Bonn during this period was depressing. Many of his colleagues in the orchestra became friends, and there were jokes and games with them. He was still able to escape from his family to the von Breunings, where he continued to enjoy comfort and cultured society. He took some courses at the new University of Bonn in 1789.

He had written more than fifty works, though none had been published yet, and he knew he was advancing in power as a musician. When Emperor Jospeh II died in 1792, Ludwig was ready to take a big step forward. A local poet wrote a memorial ode, and Beethoven set it to music as his "Cantata on the Death of Joseph II"—his first big piece, no doubt intended to establish his reputation as a composer.

The work was never performed—why, we don't know. Perhaps it was too difficult for the musical forces available; perhaps Beethoven didn't finish it in time for it to be rehearsed—in later life he seldom finished works by the deadlines, as he always had afterthoughts and improvements to add. The work was not performed until its manuscript was rediscovered in 1884, but even so it represents Beethoven's leap forward into the beginnings of an individual style. Here, for the first time, we can hear anticipations of the characteristic Beethoven sound and style, ten years before Beethoven achieved his mature style and began writing the works for which he is remembered.

Evidently he was proud of the work. We know he showed it to Joseph Haydn, who paused in Bonn on his return from his first trip to England, and no doubt it impressed Haydn: he agreed to accept Beethoven as a pupil.

Beethoven was now able to return to Vienna. His father was not well enough to be able to cause much trouble; his brothers were apprenticed to trades which could support them, Carl Caspar as a musician, Nikolaus Johann as an apothecary. Once again the Elector decided that his duty to a promising subject required him to send Ludwig to Vienna—to be taught by Haydn, since Mozart had died in December 1791. On November 1, 1792, Beethoven set off, cheered by the good wishes of his friends. All his life he kept the little album in which they wrote their good wishes for him. His aristocratic friend and patron Count Waldstein wrote, "With the help of assiduous labor you shall receive *Mozart's spirit from Haydn's hands.*" In later years Waldstein must have been pleased with his foresight.

As Beethoven left Bonn, the tidy world of his childhood was dissolving. Three years earlier a revolution had broken out in France, and disorder was beginning to spread into France's neighbors on the Rhine: the monarchs of Europe were assembling an army to rescue King Louis XVI of France and his wife, the Elector's sister, from their rebellious subjects. Beethoven's travelling coach passed through the advancing Hessian troops, off to fight the French. The Revolutionary armies, fighting for "Liberty, Equality, and Fraternity," won, and in December the Elector fled Bonn before the advancing French troops. He was restored to his capital in April 1793, and driven out again in October 1794—this time forever. The Electorate of Cologne ceased to exist.

So did Beethoven's home there. Johann van Beethoven died in Bonn December 18, 1792. Beethoven had nothing to return to, and never saw again the beautiful little city on the Rhine; but he had hopes of a great career before him in Vienna.

Passing a column of Hessians while travelling to Vienna, 1792

Chapter Three

Vienna was to be Beethoven's home for the rest of his life. A city of 200,000, the capital of the Austrian Empire drew many rich and powerful persons, a great many of whom loved music. The Emperor himself played the violin quite well, and many of his noblemen cared passionately for music. Count Andreas Razumovsky (1752-1836), for example, gave a lifetime contract to four of the finest musicians in Vienna to be his own private string quartet. They often were the first to play new works by Beethoven in later years.

These aristocratic music lovers determined the success and prosperity of Vienna's musicians. They hired musicians to perform at their parties, paid for lessons from the most successful musicians, and commissioned new pieces. Their praise made a musician famous: the public would pay to hear him perform at homes; if he toured to other cities and countries, he would attract an audience and be asked to play at the courts; and perhaps he would be commissioned to write an opera. He might even receive one of the few permanent positions—*kapellmeister* or Court Composer or court musician—which all musicians coveted.

Recommendations from Haydn, the Elector, and Count Waldstein took Beethoven into the world of the music-loving aristocracy of Vienna, and his talent established his reputation as a piano virtuoso—the best sightreader and the greatest improviser in Vienna. His style was "powerful, brilliant and imaginative"—stronger than anything that had been heard before.

With this reputation, by 1795 he was asked to play a Mozart concerto at a public concert for the benefit of Mozart's widow, and to play at a concert for Haydn. In 1796 he went on a concert tour, performing in Prague, Dresden, Leipzig, and Berlin. The King of Prussia gave him a gold snuffbox full of coins for playing.

When new rivals challenged Beethoven's first place among Vienna's pianists, he defended it. Often two rival pianists would be invited to an aristocrat's party where they would stage a sort of piano duel. Each would sightread the other's most difficult piece, improvise on a theme set by the other to show his technical and creative powers, and play a piece of his own designed to show off his greatest skills. Rival pianists staggered away defeated after Beethoven had played. His tendency to be overcome with laughter when he heard bad music made him some enemies on these occasions.

Although Beethoven valued his reputation as the finest virtuoso in Vienna, and knew that his financial success resulted from it, he was not willing to see himself as the servant or entertainer of aristocrats, as earlier musicians had done. Some of Vienna's noble music-lovers became Beethoven's friends as well as his patrons. The most important of these during the twelve years after he arrived in Vienna were Prince Karl Lichnowsky (1756-1814) and his wife Christiane (1765-1841). They gave Beethoven an apartment in their palace, and he lived with them. Beethoven said Lichnowsky treated him as "a friend and a brother," and his wife "was a second mother" to him.

How far Beethoven's talent had brought him! In Bonn he had been unable to escape being known as the son of a drunken musician; in Vienna he had become a new person, mingling on equal terms with persons of the highest rank. He even appointed one nobleman his quill-cutter-in-chief, deputizing him to trim feathers to make Beethoven's quill pens (Beethoven was clumsy and found this job difficult).

And yet he was not entirely easy in his new relationship. When he arrived in Vienna, Beethoven, chagrined by his clumsiness, took dancing lessons for a while, hoping for gracefulness and ease in society. They failed. He was uneasy about accepting too much from his new friends. Even with Lichnowsky Beethoven could be difficult. While Beethoven lived in the Lichnowsky palace, the Prince told his manservant that if he and Beethoven rang at the same time, the servant should take care of Beethoven first. When Beethoven heard this, he hired a servant for himself the same day. The Prince set aside a horse for Beethoven's use: Beethoven promptly bought a horse for himself, then forgot about it until reminded by being sent bills for its feed. Sometimes he felt he was valued only for his talent by an audience which had only a superficial appreciation of that. Once he wrote angrily to a friend, "Am I then nothing more than a music maker for yourself or the others?" He asserted his independence by refusing to perform when he was not in the mood.

Yet he was willing to accept many favors from his patrons. Probably he saw these as aid until he received some sort of permanent appointment— *kapellmeister* to some nobleman, or court composer to the Emperor. Surely his successful career would carry him to such a post: he was not yet thirty. Meanwhile, Lichnowsky gave him a quartet of fine Italian string instruments, and an annuity of 600 florins a year (about $3600) in 1800. Lichnowsky concealed other gifts. He seems to have paid for the publication of Beethoven's Opus One—his first published works, three trios, which appeared in 1795. Lichnowsky allowed Beethoven to believe that his pay came from the sale of the works.

Beethoven used his success to help his brothers. Carl Caspar came to Vienna in 1794, and made a living as a music teacher. Later he became a government clerk, probably helped by one of Beethoven's patrons. He also published a few pieces he'd composed. In 1795, when Lorenz von Breuning came to Vienna, he brought along Nikolaus Johann, who worked as an apothecary. In 1808 Ludwig was able to help him buy his own business in Linz.

While succeeding as a piano virtuoso, Beethoven was studying to improve his understanding of music and his powers as a composer. His account books for his first months in Vienna record small sums paid for coffee and chocolate with Haydn after lessons: perhaps the generous Haydn charged nothing more. Haydn loaned Beethoven money, and wrote on his behalf to the Elector, sending some pieces to show Beethoven's progress: "On the basis of these pieces, expert and amateur alike cannot but admit that Beethoven will in time become one of the greatest musical artists in Europe, and I shall be proud to call myself his teacher."

But Haydn was planning to return to England early in 1794, and was very busy. Beethoven arranged for other lessons from other composers. Johann Georg Albrechtsberger (1736-1809) taught him counterpoint, and Antonio Salieri (1750-1825), Mozart's old enemy, instructed him in vocal setting. Beethoven later dedicated works to Haydn and Salieri in gratitude for their lessons. All his teachers recognized his talent, but found him "self-willed"—always inclining to do things his own way. The music he wrote—mostly piano works and chamber music—impressed its hearers in the same way, as reflecting its creator's originality. Like Haydn, they expected great things from Beethoven in the future.

Beethoven worked hard during this period. He usually arose at daybreak, breakfasted, and worked till noon, composing or sometimes giving lessons. Apparently he was a poor teacher, impatient and unsystematic. He understood music too well to see how some ideas could be difficult for those less gifted. He never enjoyed teaching, and often postponed lessons at the last moment in order to work on a piece he was composing. One young lady, to whom Beethoven dedicated his Opus 7 piano sonata, said that Beethoven paid so little attention to teaching, that he once gave her a lesson wearing "dressing robe, slippers, and tasseled nightcap," in which unusual costume he had come across the street from his lodgings.

After he dined at noon, he took a long walk—often twice around the city. As he walked he thought about his music. He carried paper with him at all times, to write down musical ideas as they occurred to him. Some of his surviving scribbles are on music paper, some on menus. But he said these notes were only insurance, he never forgot a musical idea.

Often he worked over an idea for several years, trying many alterations in his notebooks until he was satisfied. In his surviving rough sketches and notebooks, we can follow the progression of a rough idea towards a perfection which satisfied him. His strength was not in having ideas which were perfect at first, but in being able to continue thinking about a problem until he found

Theresa von Brunswick plays for Beethoven in his be-shambled room

his solution. All his mind was applied to his work. A pupil, Ferdinand Ries, describes a walk in the country with Beethoven: "Beethoven muttered and howled the whole time, without emitting any definite notes. When I asked what he was doing he answered, 'A theme for the last *allegro* of the sonata [the *Apassionata*] has occurred to me.' When we reached the house he ran, without stopping to take off his hat, to the piano. I sat in a corner, and he soon forgot all about me. At last he got up; he was astonished to find me still there, and said, 'I cannot give you a lesson today; I must go on working.' "

After his walk he paused at a tavern to talk with friends and read the newspaper. In the evenings he was often in society, playing, or at the theatre. Usually he was in bed by ten, unless he was performing somewhere.

He enjoyed himself among friends. One says he "was droll, lively, indeed voluble at times, and fond of giving play to all the arts of wit and sarcasm, not always wisely especially in respect of political and social prejudices." In whatever company, Beethoven was always outspoken. He was fond of making rough puns, particularly on the names of friends.

His friends describe him as short, with a large head covered with thick, bristly hair, and a pockmarked, ruddy face. Beneath his broad forehead and his bushy eyebrows were the animated eyes that made his face attractive. He was often unshaven because his thick beard and his awkwardness made shaving a job he hated: he always cut himself.

When friends visited him, Beethoven liked to make coffee for them. Once he cooked a meal for some friends, but they discouraged him from ever trying that again. He was too awkward to make a good cook—clumsy at picking things up with his short, thick fingers, and forever knocking things over. The felt of his pianoforte was full of ink stains because he kept knocking the inkwell off his writing table and into the piano.

He was hard-working, strict in his principles, and demanding in his standards for himself and others. " 'As good as his word' was his favorite saying, and nothing angered him more than a broken promise." Sometimes he was so serious that he didn't realize when his leg was being pulled: a friend wrote from Berlin that a great public benefactor there had invented a lamp for the blind, and Beethoven told this exciting news to all his friends without doubting it for a moment!

His Bonn friend Franz Wegeler said that during this period, despite his work, Beethoven "was always in love," but we know nothing about the girls he may have loved. We know he was happy: he had friends, was a successful performer and a recognized composer, was composing prolifically, and his works were being published. But sometime in 1798 or 1799 he began to be annoyed by a humming or buzzing in his left ear.

Chapter Four

In April 1800 Beethoven gave his first public concert. Advertisements told the public to buy seats from the Box-keeper or from Beethoven himself in his lodgings. The program included a Mozart symphony and two arias from Haydn's *The Creation:* everything else was by Beethoven. He performed the solo part in a piano concerto, improvised on the piano, had his Septet performed—the Empress had accepted the dedication—and conducted his First Symphony, his Opus 21. The concert was a success, although a reviewer said that "the orchestra did not bother to pay any attention to the soloist" in the piano concerto, and that in the symphony "despite all efforts on the part of the conductor no fire whatsoever could be gotten out of them..."

In 1801 several important friends entered Beethoven's life. Carl Czerny (1791-1857), Beethoven's best known pupil, famous as a teacher (Franz Liszt was *his* most successful pupil) and as a composer of piano exercises for students, described years later his first meeting with Beethoven. "It was a winter's day when my father...and I took our way...to a street called *der tiefe Graben* [the deep Ditch], and climbed endless flights to the fifth and sixth story, where a rather untidy looking servant announced us to Beethoven and then admitted us. The room presented a most disorderly appearance; papers and articles of clothing were scattered about everywhere, some trunks, bare walls, hardly a chair, save the wobbly one at the Walter forte-piano (then the best), and in this room was gathered a company of from six to eight persons, among them...one of Beethoven's brothers.

"Beethoven himself wore a morning coat of some longhaired, dark grey material, and trousers to match, so that he at once recalled to me the picture in Campe's 'Robinson Cruse,' which I was reading at the time. His coal black hair cut *à la Titus*, bristled shaggily about his head. His beard—he had not been shaved for several days—made the lower part of his already brown face still darker. I also noticed with that visual quickness peculiar to children that he had cotton, which seemed to have been steeped in a yellowish liquid, in his ears.

"At that time, however, he did not give the least evidence of deafness. I was at once told to play something, and since I did not dare begin with one of his own compositions, played Mozart's great C major Concerto, the one beginning with chords. Beethoven soon gave me his attention, drew near my chair, and in those passages where I had only accompanying passages played the orchestral melody with me, using his left hand. His hands were overgrown with hair and his fingers, especially at the ends, were very broad. The satisfaction he expressed gave me the courage to play his *Sonata pathétique*, which had just appeared, and finally his "Adelaide," which my father sang in his very passable tenor. When he had ended Beethoven turned to him and said: 'The boy has talent. I will teach him myself and accept him as my pupil. Send him to me several times a week.' "

All witnesses agree with Czerny that Beethoven's lodgings were always a mess. He rarely kept a servant long because he quarrelled with them. He thought so continuously about his music that he did not notice the clutter around him. His habit of moving frequently, as his family had done during his childhood, must have made matters worse, since his possessions were rarely all unpacked, and not apt to look at home in a place where they had just arrived and from which they were likely to be moved again soon. In his thirty-five years in Vienna Beethoven lived in thirty-three places; during the summers, when he usually left town, he lived in an additional thirty-eight places.

Another important figure in Beethoven's life arrived in 1801. Ferdinand Ries (1784-1838) arrived in Vienna nearly destitute, escaping the French draft. Beethoven showed his gratitude to the Ries family for their help during his mother's last illness by taking Ferdinand as his pupil, and allowing him to perform in public as Beethoven's pupil. When the boy needed money, Beethoven loaned him some, later making it a gift. "He was really very fond of me, of which fact he once in his absent-mindedness gave me a very comical proof. Once when I returned from Silesia, (where I had spent some time at the country-seat of Prince Lichnowsky as pianist on the recommendation of Beethoven) and entered his room he was about to shave himself and had jumped up, embraced me cordially and thereby transferred so much of the lather from his left cheek to my right that he had none left. Did we laugh?"

During this period Beethoven's hearing problems worsened. At first he refused to acknowledge them, even to himself; a deaf musician, he seems to have thought, would be professionally disabled and even laughable—like a color-blind painter. When he had to admit to himself that he was having a problem, he began to discuss it with his closest friends, swearing them to secrecy. In a letter of July 1801 to a good friend, Beethoven says, "How often do I wish you were with me, for your B is living an unhappy life, quarrelling with nature and its creator, often cursing the latter for surrendering his creatures to the merest accident which often breaks or destroys the most beautiful blossoms. Know that my noblest faculty, my hearing, has greatly deteriorated...it is continually growing worse, and whether or not a cure is possible has become a question...I must stay away from everything and the most beautiful years of my life must pass by without my accomplishing all that my talent and powers bid me to do...*I beg of you to keep the matter of my deafness a profound secret to be confided to nobody, no matter whom.*"

Beethoven tried one doctor after another, impatiently rejecting their advice when no immediate improvement resulted. No one really helped. In a letter to his Bonn friend Franz Wegeler, now a doctor, Beethoven described his symptoms: "My ears sing and buzz continually, day and night. I can truly say that I am leading a wretched life. For two years I have avoided almost all social gatherings because it is impossible for me to say to people, 'I am deaf.' If I belonged to any other profession it would be easier, but in my profession it is a frightful state. Then there are my enemies, who are numerous, what would they say about this?—In order to give you an idea of this singular deafness of mine, I must tell you that in the theatre I must get very close to the orchestra in order to understand the actor, and if I am a little distant I do not hear the high tones of the instruments or singers. It is curious that in conversation there are people who do not notice my condition at all; since I have generally been absent-minded, they account for it that way. Often I can scarcely hear someone speaking softly, the tones, yes, but not the words. However, as soon as anyone shouts, it is intolerable. Heaven knows what will happen to me. *Vering says that there will be an improvement but not a complete cure*—Already I have often cursed my Creator and my existence; *Plutarch* has taught me *resignation*. If possible I will bid defiance to my fate, although there will be moments in my life when I shall be the unhappiest of God's creatures—I beg you to say nothing of my condition to anybody, not even to *Lorchen* [Wegeler's fiancée Eleonore von Breuning, Beethoven's old friend]...Resignation, what a wretched refuge, and yet the only one remaining open to me."

Poor Beethoven attempted to face his problem bravely. In November 1801 he wrote to Wegeler again, "For some time now my physical strength has been increasing more and more, and therefore my mental powers also. Every day brings me nearer to the goal which I feel but cannot describe...I will seize Fate by the throat; it shall certainly not bend and crush me completely."

But these moods alternated with despair about his condition. Beethoven usually left Vienna in summer, to live in the countryside he so loved. His doctor urged him to spare his hearing by living in a quiet place, so in April 1802 he moved to the village of Heiligenstadt, outside of Vienna, and remained there six months. Ries, one of the people to whom Beethoven had not yet admitted his problem, often came out for lessons. He would arrive at 8 A.M., and Beethoven would say, " 'Let us first take a short walk.' We went, and frequently did not return till 3 or 4 o'clock, after having made a meal in some village. On one of these wanderings Beethoven gave me the first striking proof of his loss of hearing; concerning which Stephan von Breuning had already spoken to me. I called his attention to a shepherd who was piping very agreeably in the woods on a flute made of a twig of elder. For half an hour Beethoven could hear nothing, and though I assured him that it was the same with me (which was not the case) he became extremely quiet and morose. When occasionally he seemed to be merry, it was generally to the extreme of boisterousness; but this happened seldom."

After Beethoven's death a paper was found among his belongings, his copy of a letter he had written October 6, 1802, at Heiligenstadt. It was addressed to his brother, but never sent. In this so-called "Heiligenstadt Testament" we see Beethoven wrestling with despair.

"Oh you men who think or say that I am malevolent, stubborn, or misanthropic, how greatly do you wrong me. You do not know the secret which makes me seem that way to you. From childhood on my heart and soul have been full of the tender feelings of goodwill, and I was ever inclined to accomplish great things. But, think that for six years now I have been hopelessly afflicted, made worse by senseless physicians, from year to year deceived with hopes of improvement, finally compelled to face the prospect *of a lasting malady* (whose cure will take years or, perhaps, be impossible). Though born with a fiery, active temperament, even susceptible to the diversions of society, I was soon compelled to withdraw myself, to live life alone. If at times I tried to forget all this, oh how harshly was I flung back by the doubly sad experience of my bad hearing. Yet it was impossible for me to admit an infirmity in the *one sense* which ought to be more perfect in me than in others, a sense which I once possessed in the highest perfection, a perfection such as few in my profession enjoy or ever have enjoyed.—Oh I cannot do it; therefore forgive me when you see me draw back when I would have gladly mingled with you. My misfortune is doubly painful to me because I am bound to be misunderstood; for me there can be no relaxation with my fellow men, no refined conversations, no mutual exchange of ideas. I must live almost alone, like one who has been banished; I can mix with society only as much as true necessity demands. If I approach near to people a hot terror seizes upon me, and I fear being exposed to the danger that my condition might be noticed. Thus it has been during the last six months which I have spent in the country. By ordering me to spare my hearing as much as possible, my intelligent doctor almost fell in with my own present frame of mind, though sometimes I ran counter to it by yielding to my desire for companionship. But what a humiliation for me when someone standing next to me heard a flute in the distance and *I heard nothing,* or someone heard a *shepherd singing* and again I heard nothing. Such incidents drove me almost to despair; a little more of that and I would have ended my life—it was only *my art* that held me back. Ah, it seemed to me impossible to leave the world until I had brought forth all that I felt was within me. So I endured this wretched existence—truly wretched for so susceptible a body, which can be thrown by a sudden change from the best condition to the very worst.—*Patience*, they say, is what I must now choose for my guide, and I have done so—I hope my determination will remain firm to endure until it pleases the inexorable Parcae to break the thread. Perhaps I shall get better, perhaps not; I am ready.—Forced to become a philosopher already in my twenty-eighth year,—oh, it is not easy, and for the artist much more difficult than for anyone else.—Divine One, thou seest my inmost soul; thou knowest that therein dwells the love of mankind and the desire to do good.—Oh fellow men, when at some point you read this, consider then that you have done me an injustice; someone who has had misfortune may console himself to find a similar case to his, who despite all the limitations of Nature nevertheless did everything within his powers to become accepted among worthy artists and men.—You, my brothers Carl and [Johann], as soon as I am dead, if Dr. Schmidt is still alive, ask him in my name to describe my malady, and attach this written document to his account of my illness so that as far as possible at least the world may become reconciled to me after my death.—At the same time, I declare you two to be the heirs to my small fortune (if so it can be called); divide it fairly; bear with and help each other. What injury you have done me you know was long ago forgiven. To you, brother Carl, I give special thanks for the attachment you have shown me of late. It is my wish that you may have a better and freer life than I have had. Recommend *virtue* to your children; it alone, not money, can make them happy. I speak from experience; this was what upheld me in my time of misery. Thanks to it and to my art, I did not end my life by suicide—Farewell and love each other—I thank all my friends, particularly Prince Lichnowsky and Professor Schmidt—I would like the instruments from Prince L. to be preserved by one of you, but not to be the cause of strife between you, and as soon as they can serve you a better purpose, then sell them. How happy I shall be if I can still be helpful to you in my grave—so be it.—With joy I hasten to meet death.—If it comes before I have had the chance to develop all my artistic capacities, it will still be coming too soon despite my harsh fate, and I should probably wish it later—yet even so I should be happy, for would it not free me from a state of endless suffering?—Come *when* thou wilt, I shall meet thee bravely.—Farewell and do not wholly forget me when I am dead; I deserve this from you, for during my lifetime I was thinking of you often and of ways to make you happy—please be so—" After signing and dating this on October 6, Beethoven added a postscript October 10, as he prepared to return to Vienna: 'Heiglnstadt [characteristically, he misspelled the place's name], October 10th, 1802, thus I bid thee farewell—and indeed sadly.—Yes, that fond hope—which I brought here with me, to be cured to a degree at least—this I must now wholly abandon. As the leaves of autumn fall and are withered—so likewise has my hope been blighted—I leave here—almost as I came—even the high courage—which often inspired me in the beautiful days of summer—has disappeared—Oh Providence—grant me at last but one day of pure joy—it is so long since real joy echoed in my heart—Oh when—Oh when Oh Divine One—shall I feel it again in the temple of nature and of mankind—Never?—No—Oh that would be too hard.''

Beethoven found consolation in being able to work; sometime during his crisis at Heiligenstadt he finished his cheerful Second Symphony, which reflects none of his anguish. He wrote Wegeler, "I live entirely in my music, and hardly have I completed one composition when I have already begun another. At my present rate of composing, I often produce three or four works at the same time.''

Beethoven's hearing continued to deteriorate, despite his long-held hopes of improvement. By 1810 it was poor; after 1812 it became worse; after 1816 he could no longer hear music at all, and tried to hear conversation with the aid of an ear trumpet. By 1818 he gave up even on the ear trumpet, and began to carry little notebooks—the "Conversation books"—in which his friends wrote down their remarks to him. From this point on he was essentially totally deaf.

Perhaps Beethoven's belief that a musician could not admit to deafness seems too strong to us; but we have the advantage of knowing that Beethoven proved a deaf man could still make great music. Beethoven had no example to show him it could be done. In the years ahead he created his greatest works. But his friends saw that he did not exaggerate the cost of his deafness. In 1804 Beethoven shared a lodging with his old friend Stephan von Breuning. They quarrelled fiercely, and Beethoven moved out. The quarrel ended like most of Beethoven's; he ran into Stephan accidentally, and they were reconciled. Beethoven gave Stephan his portrait. Stephan wrote to his brother-in-law Wegeler soon after, without mentioning the quarrel, but said, "You cannot conceive, my dear Wegeler, what an indescribable, I might say, fearful effect the gradual loss of his hearing has had upon him. Think of the feeling of being unhappy in one of such violent temperament; in addition, reservedness, mistrust, often towards his best friends, in many things want of decision! For the greater part, with only an occasional exception when he gives free vent to his feelings on the spur of the moment, intercourse with him is a real exertion, at which one can scarcely trust to oneself.'' Beethoven's feeling that he had been cut off from life had real causes.

Chapter Five

Beethoven had conquered despair. Having accepted his handicap, he entered his most productive years, in which he composed most of his greatest works. In the next twelve years he produced an opera, an oratorio, a mass, six symphonies, four concertos, five string quartets, three trios, three string sonatas, six piano sonatas, four sets of piano variations, many songs, incidental music for several dramas, and several symphonic overtures.

The first work in his fully mature style was his Third Symphony. Twice the length of any Mozart or Haydn symphony, this revolutionary work changed people's ideas of what a symphony could be. When Beethoven started to write it, the work was connected in his mind with new ideas as well as new forms. A friend had suggested that he should dedicate a work to Napoleon Bonaparte, the most powerful and fascinating man in Europe.

Born in Corsica, Bonaparte became an officer in the French Royal Army, survived the Revolution, and won fame as a general fighting for the Revolutionary government in Italy. In November 1799 Napoleon overthrew the corrupt existing French government and took over, calling himself First Consul—a title from the days of the Roman Republic. A generation brought up—as Beethoven had been—on Plutarch's lives of the Greek and Roman heroes found inspiration there; the French revolutionaries had seen themselves as new Romans, full of civic virtue, defending liberty against tyrants. Bonaparte, who had a genius for propaganda, used these associations. The existence of two more consuls suggested that power was divided, but Bonaparte carefully selected nonentities who wouldn't expect to do anything. Meanwhile, like Augustus Caesar, he aped republican simplicity while centralizing the government to give himself total power.

Bonaparte used his power in ways that fascinated the rest of Europe. He remade the French code of laws, ridding it of feudal leftovers. In midwinter he crossed the Alps with an army of 40,000 men to fall like a thunderbolt on the Austrian army and crush it at Marengo. Early in 1801 he compelled Austria to make a disadvantageous peace with him, then in 1802 made peace with England. All Europe was now at peace, and Napoleon had compelled the established monarchs from old dynasties to treat him as an equal.

At this point many citizens of the old monarchies admired Bonaparte. He seemed to offer a government which gave power to men of talent rather than men with famous ancestors. He looked like the most competent ruler in Europe, the most powerful, the most receptive to new ideas.

Beethoven talked about moving to Paris. Perhaps Bonaparte would reward his talents: no one in Vienna had given him the permanent post he deserved. Bonaparte's victories had attracted good composers to Paris—perhaps there Beethoven would find new music from which he could learn. Since Haydn's retirement there was no other composer in Vienna worth hearing. In fact, had Beethoven gone to Paris, he would have found a ruler with poor musical taste who only wanted short pieces to use for parades and ceremonies. Beethoven would never have written crêpe paper music—part of the decoration for big public propaganda shows.

But distance kept Beethoven from seeing Bonaparte clearly. Throughout most of 1803 he worked on his new symphony, intending to dedicate it to Bonaparte. Early in 1804 he finished it. Meanwhile Bonaparte proclaimed himself Napoleon, Emperor of the French, established his court, and brought the captive Pope to Paris to watch as he crowned himself.

Ries brought the news of Napoleon's coronation to Beethoven, who was immediately disillusioned. Realizing that Bonaparte was only another tyrant, not a ruler who would help mankind, "Beethoven went to the table, took hold of the title page...,tore it in two, and threw it on the floor."

The manuscript survives of what must have been Beethoven's draft for the copyist, a score full of erasures and corrections. On the title page is written "Sinfonia Grande Intitula Bonaparte" [Grand Symphony Titled Bonaparte.] Beethoven has erased the last two words so violently that his eraser dug a hole in the paper where "Bonaparte" had been. Instead the symphony was published with the inscription, "to celebrate the memory of a great man," and the work was dedicated to Prince Lobkowitz, who had it performed privately. The symphony is now known as the "Eroica," and is indeed heroic music, full of energy and movement, surging forward. The public did not get to hear it until 1805, and many of them were perplexed by its novelty; one critic complained, "often it loses itself in lawlessness."

Hereafter Beethoven's attitude to Bonaparte was ambivalent: at one point he is supposed to have said, "It's a pity I do not understand the art of war as well as I do the art of music. I would conquer him!" And yet he still played with the idea of going to Paris.

No one in Europe could escape being fascinated and affected by the long skyrocket-burst of Bonaparte's career. This egocentric gangster knocked over the kingdoms of Europe like ninepins, and the whims of his quest for glory began wars which led to death or injury for millions. The mere passage of his armies caused some to starve, while others grew rich by selling needed supplies to the armies. (Beethoven's brother Johann became well-to-do this way.)

The new Emperor's successes affected Beethoven's next major work, though when he began thinking of composing an opera, he can hardly have expected the affairs of monarchs to interfere with its success. In 1803 the impresario Emanuel Shikaneder offered Beethoven the chance to conduct a concert in his new Theatre-an-der-Wien whenever he chose; meanwhile, Beethoven was to write him an opera.

In April 1803 Beethoven did give a concert at the theatre. The program included the First and Second Symphonies, the Third Piano Concerto, and a new oratorio, *Christ on the Mount of Olives*, written especially for this concert. The performance had to be postponed one day, probably because Beethoven hadn't finished. At five A.M. the day of the concert Ries found Beethoven in bed, writing out the trombone parts for the orchestra. The rehearsal began at eight A.M., and went terribly—the musicians were playing scores they'd never seen, and whenever a wrong note was played Beethoven had to find out if the error was the player's or a copyist's mistake in the score. There must have been constant stopping, arguing, and starting again. By two in the afternoon everyone was tired, angry, and depressed. Prince Lichnowsky, who had sat patiently through the rehearsal, sent out for food and wine for the musicians, which helped everyone's temper a great deal, and they went through the oratorio once more before the concert began at six.

The oratorio was not the only piece finished at the last moment. Beethoven asked Ignaz von Seyfried to turn the pages for him as he played the piano part of the concerto. "But—heaven help me! —that was easier said than done. I saw almost nothing but empty leaves; at the most on one page or the other a few Egyptian hieroglyphs wholly unintelligible to me scribbled down to serve as clues for him; for he played nearly all of the solo part from memory, since, as was so often the case, he had not had time to put it all down on paper. He gave me a secret glance whenever he was at the end of one of the invisible passages and my scarcely concealable anxiety not to miss the decisive moment amused him greatly and he laughed heartily at the jovial supper which we ate afterwards."

Seyfried says that with Beethoven's style of conducting the other pieces on the program, "the orchestra always had to have a care in order not to be led astray by its mentor; for he had ears only for his composition and was ceaselessly occupied by manifold gesticulations to indicate the desired expression. He often made a down beat for an accent in the wrong place. [One cause of the eccentricity of his conducting, of course, was his progressive inability to hear the orchestra. At this point Beethoven was still concealing his deafness.] He used to suggest a *diminuendo* by crouching down more and more, and at a *pianissimo* he would almost creep under the desk. When the volume of sound grew he rose up also as if out of a stage-trap, and with the entrance of the power of the band he would stand upon the tips of his toes almost as big as a giant, and waving his arms, seemed about to soar upwards to the skies."

Beethoven was unwilling to make the players repeat passages which went badly. " 'It will go better next time,' he would say. He was very particular about expression, the delicate nuances, the equable distribution of light and shade as well as an effective *tempo rubato*, and without betraying vexation, would discuss them with the individual players. When he then observed that the players would enter into his intentions and play together with increasing ardor, inspired by the magical power of his creations, his face would be transfigured with joy, all his features beamed pleasure and satisfaction, a pleased smile would play around his lips and a thundering *'Bravi tutti!'* reward the successful achievement."

Odd conducting ways, like leaping into the air

Chapter Six

When he had given this concert and finished the "Eroica," Beethoven settled down to writing his opera. He selected a play which had recently succeeded in France, *Leonore, or Conjugal Love*, by J.N. Bouilly, to provide his story. (Operas, like movies and television shows nowadays, usually recycled stories which had already made money for someone else.) Joseph von Sonnleithner, Secretary of the Court Theatres, put the story into German for him.

The play was one of a number of recent French plays on the subject of a rescue from prison. With first one party in power, then another, during the bloody revolutions of the last fifteen years, most Frenchmen had been deeply interested in someone's chances of getting out of prison. But all the countries of Europe had political prisons, and political prisoners in them.

The story of *Leonore*, which we know today as *Fidelio*, is simple. Fidelio, the new assistant to head-jailor Rocco, is actually Leonore, a woman in disguise, seeking her husband Florestan, who had disappeared. Pizarro, the governor of the prison, asks Rocco to help him dispose of the prisoner in the deepest dungeon before a prison inspector arrives. The prisoner is Pizarro's personal enemy, imprisoned without any legal cause. Rocco recoils in horror from the idea of murdering the prisoner, but agrees to dig a grave in the cell.

Rocco takes Fidelio to help him in the dark dungeon of the unknown prisoner. Leonore hopes and fears that this will be her husband. It is! But she is there to dig his grave, and he is nearly dead from starvation. She gives him food, then pulls a pistol and defies Pizarro when he comes to murder Florestan. A trumpet is heard: Don Fernando, the Minister who is inspecting the prison, has arrived. Florestan is saved! Don Fernando will see that justice is done to all the prisoners: Florestan, saved by his wife's devotion, is released, and Pizarro is arrested.

Sonnleithner attempted to prevent objections by the Austrian state censors to the political implications of the story by setting it in the sixteenth century in Spain. Pizarro is an unjust individual who betrays his trust, but the government itself serves justice. The censors still objected, feeling that any drama which portrayed the release of prisoners with approval was probably revolutionary in sentiment. Sonnleithner finally won approval by telling the censors that the opera was going to be performed for the Empress, who liked the story very much. That worked.

The dangerous political implications of the story were what had attracted Beethoven, who hated all the forces which imprison the spirit of mankind—arbitrary power, tyranny, ignorance, intolerance. One of the profoundly moving moments in *Fidelio* comes when Fidelio persuades Rocco to allow the prisoners to come out of their cells for air and exercise in the yard: they emerge into the unaccustomed daylight in a miniature liberation, singing a chorus which swells from a hushed noise to a rejoicing in "God's light" that frightens the jailors into reimprisoning them. Beethoven shows man's spirit surviving imprisonment, ready for resurrection. He hoped to see mankind liberated through Enlightenment, brotherhood, and benevolence. Beethoven himself tried in his own life to rescue others—his father and his brothers, and later his nephew. Perhaps he thought also of being released from the prison of his deafness.

Beethoven found equally moving Leonore's devotion to her husband. Her settled married love, based on morality, is strong enough to defeat even a prison. No doubt he wondered as he wrote, would he ever find his own Leonore?

Beethoven started writing his opera in January 1804, expecting to finish in June. But, as was so often the case, he found himself taking longer than he had intended because he was determined to get things just right. He worked painstakingly: for one example, in his sketchbook there are eighteen different beginnings for Florestan's despairing aria in his dungeon. No wonder he did not finish until late in 1805.

Meanwhile a new war with Napoleon broke out. By July there were food shortages and food riots in Vienna—all the food was going to supply the Austrian army. While the Austrian censors worried whether public performance of *Leonore* would be dangerous for the state, Napoleon's army reached the Danube. After a disastrous Austrian defeat at Ulm, nothing stood between Napoleon and Vienna.

Leonore was now in rehearsal. The cast was uneven: most of the good male singers had left Vienna, no doubt in fear of being drafted into the French army—a fate that overtook Ries. Banks closed, and the well-to-do left Vienna. During the last week of rehearsals the French occupied Vienna. Troops were quartered in the houses of the citizens, and were looting in the streets.

Beethoven had been very nervous as his opera was rehearsed. When the third bassoonist missed one rehearsal, Beethoven fussed and fretted. Lobkowitz, who was with him, told him not to worry—how much difference could a missing third bassoonist make? Beethoven resented this remark all evening; on the way home, still fuming, as he passed the Lobkowitz Palace he put his head in the front door to yell into the reception hall, "Lobkowitzian ass!" A few days later the French commander of the city took Lobkowitz's palace for his headquarters.

A small orchestra tried out the overture privately at Lichnowsky's: it was agreed that it was too frivolous to suit the drama, and Beethoven composed another. (The first is now known as Leonore Overture No. 1, the second as Leonore No. 2.)

At the last moment the manager of the theatre decided that the opera should be called *Fidelio*, not *Leonore*—which annoyed Beethoven. At the premiere on November 20, the house was nowhere near full. Many of Beethoven's usual patrons had left the city, or were afraid to come out in public. Many of the spectators were French soldiers, who probably didn't understand the German text. The audience was bored. At the second performance leaflets with verses praising Beethoven were showered from the balcony: Stephan von Breuning wrote the verses, and arranged the distribution. But this didn't help the opera, and after one more performance, the management dropped it.

Within two weeks Napoleon defeated the Austrians and Russians decisively at Austerlitz. He dictated peace on his own terms, taking about a hundred million dollars and 400 great paintings from Austria's palaces. Austria doubled its taxes, and all citizens were taxed half a year's rent.

As Beethoven's friends could do nothing about Napoleon, they turned to salvaging *Fidelio*. Stephan von Breuning suggested changes and cuts in the libretto, as everyone agreed the opera was too long. In December Prince Lichnowsky called Beethoven's friends together for a private performance of the opera at his palace, after which changes would be discussed. Princess Lichnowsky played the score on the piano, accompanied by the orchestra leader Clement on the violin, as the singers went through the opera. The Prince, Beethoven, his brother Carl Caspar, von Breuning, and some musician friends listened.

Afterwards, when his friends urged Beethoven to accept certain cuts so that the first two acts could be condensed into one, Beethoven resisted. A singer from the cast says, "Yet he defended every measure, and did so with such nobility and artistic dignity that I was ready to kneel at his feet. But when he came to the chief point...which would make it possible to fuse the two acts into one, he was beside himself, shouted uninterruptedly, 'Not a note!' and tried to run off with his score. But the Princess laid her hands, folded as though in prayer, on the score entrusted to her, looked up with indescribable mildness at the angry genius and behold—his rage melted at her glance, and he once more resignedly resumed his place."

As Beethoven resisted every change, it took the company from seven at night until one in the morning to persuade him to cut three numbers from his

Beethoven conducting *Fidelio*, November 20, 1805

opera. He finally yielded to please Princess Lichnowsky. Then supper was served—"then none was happier and gayer than Beethoven."

But within a few days he changed his mind again, putting the numbers back in, making two alternate cuts instead. More revisions followed: the orchestra had messed up one difficult passage in the overture. Instead of chnaging that, Beethoven decided to rewrite the whole overture: he came up with the wonderful Leonore No. 3. He wanted the title changed back to *Leonore:* it was agreed upon, then not done. The opera was reduced from three to two acts, then put on the stage again, with some improvements in the cast. It was performed March 19, 1806 and again April 10. The critics liked it better, but Beethoven was angry with the orchestra's performance: "All delight in composing departs when one hears one's music played *thus!*" he wrote to an official of the theatre. Finally, he became suspicious that he was not getting his agreed-upon share of the box-office takings, quarrelled with the Director of the theatre, and walked out with his score. No more performances of *Fidelio* were given. Beethoven himself was still not satisfied with his opera.

The Prince and Princess Lichnowsky
plead in vain with Beethoven

Chapter Seven

Fidelio's failure wounded Beethoven doubly: its hearers had rejected a work he cared about, the best he could make; also, the time he had spent composing the opera would bring in no money, and probably he would not be asked to write another opera. (In fact, while he talked about composing another opera, he never chose a libretto: perhaps the failure of this one had been so unpleasant he did not wish to repeat the experience.) One way of becoming well-to-do as a composer—the way of Handel and Gluck—had closed itself to him.

In March 1808 Beethoven went to a concert given to honor Haydn's seventy-sixth birthday. Haydn was carried into the hall on a stretcher. Old, weak, and thin, he shrank from the noise of the audience's applause. At the end of the first part of the program he fainted and had to be taken home. Beethoven came up to Haydn as he was about to leave, knelt beside him, and kissed his hand. Seeing him so weak, unable to compose, must have led Beethoven to think about his own future.

He was now in his late thirties. His deafness was increasing: he would not be able to make money by performing as a pianist, or by conducting, or by teaching. What would he live on when he became unable to work?

At this time Beethoven made several efforts to secure his financial future. In 1807 Prince Nicholas Esterhazy, who had commissioned Haydn's late masterpieces, the annual masses, asked Beethoven to replace Haydn in writing a Mass to honor the Prince's wife. Beethoven labored carefully on this Mass: he even managed, uncharacteristically, to finish it by the deadline. Perhaps it occurred to him the Esterhazy family could make him secure, as it had Haydn. But when Beethoven journeyed to Eisenstadt to conduct the performance, he was given inferior lodgings, the Prince indicated that he did not understand or like the work, and the Prince's *Kapellmeister* laughed. Beethoven left, angry and disappointed, and did not give the Prince the score of the Mass or dedicate the work to him. The work was not published for several years.

In 1806 Beethoven had quarrelled fiercely with a more reliable patron, Prince Lichnowsky. The Prince urged Beethoven to improvise for some French officers, his guests; Beethoven was not in the mood and grew angry. Leaving the house in a huff, he went home and dashed on to the floor a bust of the Prince which had been a gift to him. It broke. He is supposed to have written to his patron, "Prince, what you are you are by accident of birth; what I am I am through myself. There have been and will still be thousands of princes; there is only one Beethoven." The quarrel must have reminded him that even the best patron might cease to support an artist.

34

Young LUDWIG VAN BEETHOVEN
after Willibord Joseph Mähler, 1804/5

Soon after the fiasco of the Esterhazy Mass, an offer came which seemed as if it might provide the security Beethoven wanted. Napoleon had made his younger brother King Jerome of Westphalia—a new German state, constructed out of pieces taken from defeated states. In October 1808 King Jerome asked Beethoven to become his *Kapellmeister* in his capital of Cassel. In exchange for conducting at the King's rare concerts, he would be given a salary of 600 ducats and a travel allowance. It is hard to compare the values of money then and now, but the offer was princely—probably the equivalent of $20,000 or more now, with the possibility that Beethoven could continue to make as much as he was already making from the sale of his works.

But Beethoven didn't want to go to the small town of Cassel to dangle in attendance on a petty Bonaparte who didn't much care about music. Also, Beethoven must have known that he was not likely to be happy running an orchestra, or to do the job well.

Instead, he used King Jerome's offer to shame the Viennese into providing some guarantee of his future. Several of his patrons felt that Vienna would be disgraced if it let Beethoven leave. After negotiating with an agent of Beethoven's, three of his patrons agreed "to place Herr Ludwig van Beethoven in a position where the necessaries of life shall not cause him embarrassment or clog his powerful genius," by providing him a pension of 4000 florins a year for life, even if he was too ill to work—over $30,000 today. The pension would end if Beethoven obtained a proper court position or left Austria.

All three patrons were younger than Beethoven—older music lovers often found his music too new, too disturbing. Two of them—Archduke Rudolph (1788-1832), the Emperor's brother and a pupil of Beethoven's since 1803, and Prince Kinsky (1781-1812)—were in their twenties. The third was Beethoven's old friend Prince Lobkowitz (1772-1816). They offered him more money than King Jerome had, and required less work of him. Their generosity shows that sometimes the old aristocratic system of patronage worked well— when the aristocrats had artistic knowledge and a belief in their responsibility to support talent. The pension is also a tribute to Beethoven: it shows the great value placed upon his talents and the confidence of the donors that Beethoven would use any money given him for the purpose intended—to compose.

The arrangement seemed to offer Beethoven the greatest independence possible within the system of patronage. Now he should be free to compose with a tranquil mind. But once again Napoleon upset his life: French armies invaded Austria again. Beethoven received his pension in late February 1809; by May the Imperial Family had fled Vienna, the French army was besieging and shelling the city, and Beethoven had taken refuge with his brother Carl

Vienna, 1809

Caspar's family in their cellar. On May 31, during this turmoil, old Haydn died. The French occupied the city again. Beethoven wrote, "What a destructive, disorderly life I see and hear around me; nothing but drums, cannon and human misery in every form."

Austria paid for its defeat by cheating its people. In March 1811 the state devalued its currency, which lost four-fifths of its official value. Suddenly Beethoven's pension was no longer a princely sum, and soon the devalued currency lost even more of its worth.

In fact, he wasn't even getting his pension. The devaluation had affected his patrons, too. Prince Lobkowitz had been forced to realize that he was nearly bankrupt; his affairs were put in the hands of a financial manager, who reorganized them. For four years his pension wasn't paid. Beethoven sued, but got no satisfaction. He also appealed to his patrons to adjust the sum paid to him to make it equal in value to what he had been promised. Archduke Rudolph agreed, and paid his share regularly. Prince Kinsky agreed belatedly, then died in a riding accident in 1812. His estate failed to pay Beethoven anything for three years. Lobkowitz finally settled in 1814. From 1815 on Beethoven received 3,400 florins a year from his pension—about $6,000 now.

Even before the confusing devaluation, Beethoven found it difficult to understand his own finances. As a schoolboy his arithmetic had been poor; in his adult account books the figures are often added up incorrectly. Ries says, "Beethoven knew scarcely anything about money, because of which he had frequent quarrels, since he was always mistrustful, and frequently thought himself cheated when it was not the case. Easily excited, he called people cheats, for which in the case of waiters he had to make good with tips. At length his peculiarities and absent-mindedness became known in the inns which he frequented most often and he was permitted to go in his way even when he went without paying the bill."

Some of Beethoven's ill humor in matters dealing with money must be attributed to the frustration anyone feels when forced to deal with matters he does not understand (see how many people get testy at income tax time); then too Beethoven's deafness cut him off, and led him to suspect other people of trying to take advantage of him. Straining to hear what people said to him and fearing that they were deceiving him or making fun of him, Beethoven sometimes gave way to violent outbreaks of temper. His strong words and actions lasted a short time, and were often followed by an apology. He must, as his deafness increased, have looked forward joylessly to a period when he would be cut off from all social communication. No doubt this was one reason why he wanted to marry, or to love, to behave like everyone else in the human race, before it was too late.

Chapter Eight

During the French occupation in 1809 a young French diplomat who loved music called on Beethoven. Everyone had warned him that Beethoven was a bear, and would not receive him; instead Beethoven took a liking to him. "[Beethoven's] lodging, I believe, consisted of only two rooms, the first one having an alcove containing the bed, but small and dark, for which reason he made his toilet in the second room, or salon. Picture to yourself the dirtiest, most disorderly place imaginable—blotches of moisture covered the ceiling; an oldish grand piano, on which the dust disputed the place with various pieces of engraved and manuscript music; under the piano (I do not exaggerate) an unemptied chamber pot; beside it, a small walnut table accustomed to the frequent overturning of the writing materials placed upon it; a quantity of pens encrusted with ink, compared wherewith the proverbial tavern-pens would shine; then more music. The chairs, mostly cane-seated, were covered with plates bearing the remains of last night's supper, and with wearing apparel, etc."

No doubt Beethoven was sometimes tired of living in such squalor. He hired servants, whom he suspected of cheating him and soon fired again, but had too little attention to spare to supervise them. His brother Carl Caspar had married Johanna Riess, the daughter of a well-to-do upholsterer, May 25, 1806. Although Beethoven had opposed the marriage at the time (he always felt it his duty to tell his brothers what to do) and had quarrelled with his brother, he soon became reconciled and visited there often. Karl, the only child of this marriage, was born September 4, 1806, and Beethoven soon became fond of him. Carl Caspar and his wife had a typical Beethoven family marriage—stormy, with violent quarrels and equally violent reunions.

In spite of their example Beethoven hoped he could increase his comfort and decrease his loneliness by marrying. He had thought of marriage before: we think he proposed during the 1790's to a singer, Magdalena Willman, who refused him. In 1810 he proposed marriage again—this time to young Therese Malfatti, only nineteen, the daughter of Beethoven's physician. Beethoven had adopted the Malfattis as a sort of substitute family; he was friendly with Therese, who liked him and knew music well enough to admire his talents; but she was not willing to marry him. Probably she was wise: Beethoven would not have been easy to live with.

Perhaps Beethoven was somewhat relieved to be refused. He must have known that marriage would require many changes in him; something would have to be as important as his work. Perhaps he feared he could not make a woman happy. Most of his romantic attachments seem to have been to women who were married to or in love with friends of his. Beethoven would not make himself a friend's rival; he could love safely, without the responsibility of having his love returned. But in one case we know that a love affair went beyond this safe point, and he experienced the greatest love of his life.

We know about this love only because after Beethoven's death his executors discovered several documents of great importance to him, which he had kept in a secret drawer: one was the Heiligenstadt Testament, another a long love letter. After much argument scholars have established that it was written at the spa of Teplitz in what is now Czechoslovakia in 1812.

> July 6, in the morning
>
> My angel, my all, my very self—
>
> Only a few words today and at that with pencil (with yours)—Not till tomorrow will my lodgings be definitely determined upon—what a useless waste of time—Why this deep sorrow when necessity speaks—can our love endure except through sacrifices, through not demanding everything from one another; can you change the fact that you are not wholly mine, I not wholly thine—Oh God, look out into the beauties of nature and comfort yourself with that which must be—Love demands everything and that very justly—*thus it is to me with you, and to you with me.* If only you do not forget that I must live *for me and for you;* if we were wholly united you would feel the pain of it as little as I—...We shall surely see each other soon; moreover, today I cannot share with you the thoughts I have had during the last few days touching my own life—If our hearts were always close together, I would have none of these. My heart is so full of so many things to say to you—ah—there are moments when I feel that speech amounts to nothing at all—Cheer up—remain my true love, my only love, my all as I am yours. The gods must send us the rest, what for us must and shall be—
>
> Your faithful Ludwig"

Beethoven continued the letter, having learned that he could not mail it until Thursday, when the mail coach went to Karlsbad:

> Though still in bed, my thoughts go out to you, my Eternally Beloved, now and then joyfully, then sadly, waiting to learn whether or not fate will hear us—I can live only wholly with you or not at all...my life in V[ienna] is now a wretched life—Your love makes me at once the happiest and the unhappiest of men—At my age I need a steady, quiet life—can that be so in our connection? My angel, I have just been told that the mail-coach goes every day—and I must close at once so that you may receive the letter at once.—Be calm, only by a calm consideration of our existence can we achieve our purpose

to live together—Be calm—love me—today—yesterday—Oh continue to love me—never misjudge the most faithful heart of your beloved.

> ever thine
> ever mine
> ever ours   L."

Each Beethoven scholar suggests a different woman as Beethoven's beloved; but we don't really need to know who she was. The letter makes it clear that he loved her most passionately, that for once he was loved passionately in return, and that some obstacle prevented their being together. Most probably the lady was already married. Beethoven had been attracted several times to women who were attached to friends of his, but had not formed any relationship. In this case, however, matters evidently went much further. Perhaps he is considering the possibility of living with his beloved: will she interfere with his work? Selfish? If Beethoven was not entitled to consider his work important, who is? While he seems slightly afraid of the consequences of this love, it is clear that he derived a great deal of joy and some pain from it, and that it lived up to his standards—spiritual as well as physical. He wrote later in a notebook, "Sensual union without a union of souls is bestial and will always remain so." In this affair he came as close as he was ever to come to finding a Leonore of his own, a love as true and heroic as the one he had imagined in his opera.

But his love affair caused Beethoven frustration as well as joy, and this frustration accounts in part for his actions during a visit in September to his brother Johann in Linz. Beethoven was outraged at finding that his brother, now thirty-five, a successful apothecary, had made his housekeeper Therese Obermeyer his mistress. Unable to achieve a lawful relationship himself, Beethoven would not tolerate his brother's unlawful one. He told Johann to break off the affair; Johann told Ludwig to mind his own business. Beethoven now went to the local Bishop and the police, and complained about his brother's conduct; the police, who enforced morality when anyone insisted they should, gave an order to banish the girl from Linz from a certain day. Johann prevented this by marrying Therese in November, enraging Beethoven further. But Beethoven had driven him into it. Unfortunately the marriage was not a happy one; many quarrels occurred. Evidently the Beethoven brothers were not easy husbands.

Amid all this turmoil Beethoven seems to have finished his Eighth Symphony in Linz. The agitations of his daily life did not necessarily affect his creative life.

Chapter Nine

Having given up the idea of finding happiness through love, Beethoven expected to find it only in his work. In his day book he wrote, *"Thou mayest no longer be a man, not for thyself, only for others, for thee there is no happiness except in thyself, in thy art*—O God, give me strength to conquer myself, nothing must chain me to life."

In compensation, chance gave Beethoven his greatest popular and financial success at this period—indirectly, through Napoleon, whose attack on Russia in 1812 had ended in disaster. Winter ruined his army, and only 15% of the 400,000 men he took into Russia returned alive. As Napoleon's weakness began to show, the European powers he had dominated turned on him. The English army commanded by the Duke of Wellington beat the French army in Spain decisively at Vittoria June 21, 1813; by August Austria joined the coalition against Napoleon, and in October the allied armies of Russia, Prussia, Austria, and Sweden defeated Napoleon himself decisively in the "Battle of the Nations" at Leipzig.

As Napoleon fell, Austria rose; and with its success rose the patriotism of its citizens, now they had something to cheer about. An acquaintance of Beethoven's, Johann Nepomuk Mälzel (1772-1838), was eager to profit from this surge of patriotism. Mälzel was a sort of musical mechanic, experimenting with machine-made music. His mechanical trumpeter had had a great success, aided by Mälzel's skill in blowing his own horn; now he had developed the "Mechanical Panharmonicon," a device able to play tunes with all the instruments of a military band. Different cylinders played different pieces in this ancestral jukebox.

Mälzel made some ear trumpets for Beethoven, with the aid of which Beethoven's friends could bellow into his better ear. He suggested that if Beethoven wrote a piece for the Panharmonicon, they could both make some money. If the piece was patriotic, they could both make a lot of money. He gave Beethoven a preliminary scenario for a piece celebrating Wellington's victory at Vittoria, packed full of easily recognizable national airs. The British troops enter to trumpets, drums, and "Rule, Britannia"; then here come the French, to *"Malbrouk s'en va-t'en guerre,"* better known to us in its English versions as "For he's a jolly good fellow," or "The bear went over the mountain." Then comes the battle, very jolly and stirring, followed with a "Symphony of Victory" including "God Save the King." Beethoven, amused, wrote this; now Mälzel had another idea: the piece could be orchestrated instead for a full orchestra, and would draw crowds to a major concert. Beethoven agreed.

Beethoven after W. J. Mähler, 1815

Mälzel got state permission to give two concerts for the benefit of widows and orphans of Austrian soldiers; he hoped that after a success he could arrange more concerts for the benefit of Mälzel and Beethoven. They collected an orchestra of the most important musicians of Vienna, most of whom, like Beethoven, regarded "Wellington's Victory" as a stupendous musical joke on anyone who took it seriously. The concert's program began with the Beethoven Seventh Symphony, heard for the first time; went on to two marches played by Mälzel's Mechanical Trumpeter, backed by the full orchestra; and concluded with "Wellington's Victory." Everything was a great success, and the audience insisted on hearing the Allegretto of the symphony again.

Beethoven, overjoyed by his success, now dumped poor Mälzel and gave a new concert in early January 1814, replacing the Mechanical Trumpeter with some of his incidental music for theatre, and drawing audience applause by suddenly unveiling a bust of the Austrian Emperor during the finale of the battle symphony. The performance was a success again, in spite of Beethoven's attempt to conduct. He was now so deaf that he could not tell what the orchestra was doing. When he had the players thoroughly confused, the concertmaster took over directing them, and not for some time did Beethoven notice the change. Again the audience encored some sections.

This success led to proposals for further concerts, and the suggestion that it was time to revive *Fidelio*. Beethoven said he would not have the opera performed again unless he could revise it. He asked his friend Georg Treitschke (1776-1842), stage manager and manager of the theatre, to revise the libretto. The work was shortened, and Beethoven rewrote many sections. One was a new aria for Florestan, starving in despair in his dungeon. Treitschke describes the writing of this aria: "Beethoven came to me about seven o'clock in the evening. After we had discussed other things, he asked how matters stood with the aria? It was just finished, I handed it to him. He read, ran up and down the room, muttered, growled, as was his habit instead of singing—and tore open the pianoforte. My wife had often vainly begged him to play; to-day he placed the text in front of him and began to improvise marvellously—music which no magic could hold fast. Out of it he seemed to conjure the motive of the aria. The hours went by, but Beethoven improvised on. Supper, which he had purposed to eat with us, was served, but he would not permit himself to be disturbed. It was late when he embraced me, and declining the meal, he hurried home. The next day the admirable composition was finished."

In late February Beethoven gave another concert. As usual, he overloaded the program, which included the Seventh Symphony, a new terzetto, the première of the Eighth Symphony, and the inevitable "Wellington's Victory." Although the audience was too surfeited to take in the Eighth Symphony, they were enthusiastic, and the hall was full. After the concert, when Beethoven got some cherries from a couple of girls who were selling them outside, they refused his money and one said, "I'll take nothing from you We saw you in the Redoutensaal when we heard your beautiful music." Beethoven must have enjoyed this: he told the story to many of his friends.

Meanwhile, Mälzel, who felt, reasonably enough, that he had been treated unfairly, hired a lawyer and tried to reclaim some rights in "Wellington's Victory." Beethoven refused any agreement; Mälzel managed to put together a score of his own, with which he produced two concerts in Munich for his own benefit. Beethoven, enraged, sued him—to no effect. As usual with Beethoven's quarrels, this all ended in a reconciliation: a few years later each paid half the legal costs. Mälzel perfected his most important invention, the metronome, in 1817, and Beethoven wrote a testimonial for it, and put metronome markings into his scores. Mälzel became wealthy, and moved to the United States.

The revision of *Fidelio* moved slowly with all these distractions. As usual, the more things Beethoven fixed, the more things seemed to need work. Although the first performance was scheduled for May 23, the promised new overture had not been written for the final rehearsal on the 22nd. Beethoven dined with a friend at an inn. After dinner he took the menu, drew lines on the blank side, and began to write. "Come, let's go," his friend said. "No, wait a little; I have an idea for my overture," said Beethoven, who remained to finish his sketch.

Treitschke says, "The orchestra was called to rehearsal on the morning of the performance. B. did not come. After waiting a long time we drove to his lodgings to bring him, but—he lay in bed, sleeping soundly, beside him stood a goblet with wine and a biscuit in it, the sheets of the overture were scattered on the bed and floor. A burnt-out candle showed that he had worked far into the night. The impossibility of completing the overture was plain..."For the opening night of this third version of *Fidelio* an irrelevant older overture was used instead of any of the three Leonore Overtures or the new Fidelio Overture.

Third time lucky: this time *Fidelio* was a success. It achieved twenty performances that year, one of which was a benefit for Beethoven, and very profitable. He must have regretted, however, the death of his old friend Prince Lichnowsky in April—a month and a half too soon to see the final triumph of an opera he had believed in.

Payment refused

46

After the defeated Napoleon abdicated in April 1814 the triumphant allies agreed on a grand conference in Vienna to reshape Europe. Countries which had supported Napoleon were to be punished; those who had fought against him were to be rewarded with new territory; and the rulers who had fled from the armies of the French Revolution and of Napoleon were to be restored to their thrones, whether deserving or not—unless some more powerful country wanted their territory. Beethoven was set to work writing a cantata celebrating this gathering, to be called "The Glorious Moment." Neither its text nor its music are glorious.

But the visiting monarchs dressed up his audiences, and drew crowds of citizens eager to cheer for victory and gape at rulers. In September *Fidelio* was performed for an audience including the Kings of Denmark, Prussia, and Wurtemberg, and the Czar of Russia. At Beethoven's November concert again many visiting sovereigns were in the audience. (The King of Prussia left early, however.) The program offered the first performance of the cantata, and included the Seventh Symphony and the inevitable "Wellington's Victory." This program was repeated twice more before the year's end.

Five of the eleven concerts Beethoven gave in his lifetime took place in this year of his glory. From them he made enough money to buy seven shares in a bank. Early in 1815 the irritating matter of his pension was settled. It seemed he could look forward to financial security and public triumphs in the Vienna which made him an Honorary Citizen for his service to its charities.

But in fact this year of successes marked the end of Beethoven's most popular period. Even though the Congress of Vienna tried to put the world back together as it had been before the French Revolution, it could not repeal change. Few aristocrats could still afford to maintain musical establishments. Beethoven's patrons were disappearing. Kinsky had died in 1812, Lichnowsky in 1814, and Lobkowitz would die in 1816. Razumovsky returned to Russia after his Viennese palace burned. Only Archduke Rudolph remained a reliable patron: ultimately fifteen Beethoven works were dedicated to him.

The postwar audience seemed to want exciting dance music, good comic operas, and operas with displays of vocal pyrotechnics. Vienna went wild over the waltz and the operas of Rossini. Beethoven was not interested in writing such works, and as he moved towards a new style, he was not writing works in the popular forms most desired by publishers. Between 1812 and 1824 the public heard no new symphony from him; after 1809 there were no more concertos. Between 1809 and 1823 there were no piano variations. Also new family responsibilities gave him less time to compose and made him less productive in the period ahead.

Chapter Ten

In November 1815 Beethoven's brother Carl Caspar, who had been ill with tuberculosis for some time, realized that he was dying. He had often quarrelled with his wife Johanna—at one point he had even denounced her to the police for stealing money from him, and she had been sentenced to stay in her own house for a month. His harsh ideas of discipline had often led him to beat his son Karl, who was now nine. But he loved them, and he wanted to assure their future.

On November 14, the day before Carl Caspar died, he made his will, dividing his property equally between Johanna and Karl. He did not trust her to manage the property and the boy's education wisely, so he made his brother Ludwig co-guardian with Johanna. Ludwig protested: he had never thought well of Johanna, and did not "wish to be bound up with such a bad woman in a matter of such importance as the education of the child." Carl Caspar revised his will, making Ludwig sole guardian; now Johanna protested at having no right over the future of her own child. Depressed by this squabbling, tired out, and fearful of the future, Carl Caspar added a codicil to his will: "Having learned that my brother, Herr Ludwig van Beethoven, desires after my death to take wholly to himself my son Karl, and wholly to withdraw him from the supervision and training of his mother, and inasmuch as the best of harmony does not exist between my brother and my wife, I have found it necessary to add to my will that I by no means desire that my son be taken away from his mother, but that he shall always and so long as his future career permits remain with his mother, to which end the guardianship of him is to be exercised by her as well as my brother. Only by unity can the object which I had in view in appointing my brother guardian of my son be attained, wherefore, for the welfare of my child, I recommend *compliance* to my wife and more *moderation* to my brother. God permit them to be harmonious for the sake of my child's welfare. This is the last wish of the dying husband and brother."

Carl Caspar's touching last request was in vain. The tug-of-war between Ludwig and Johanna for possession of Karl which started over Carl Caspar's deathbed continued for the next eleven years, and stretched poor Karl nearly to the breaking point. His uncle and his mother also suffered a great deal of anger, frustration, and grief during the struggle.

Early in 1816 Beethoven went to court to have Johanna excluded as his co-guardian, claiming that she was of bad moral character and had forced Carl Caspar to write the codicil. He had never had to work with a woman,

Johann van Beethoven

Beethoven arguing with his sister-in-law over Karl

and neither knew how, nor wished to, particularly with the forceful, emotional Johanna, whom he had always distrusted. He even suspected her, quite unjustly, of having poisoned her husband.

Beethoven's statements about Johanna are often irrational and unfair. He refers to her as Minerva, Circe, Medea, the Queen of the Night...Instead of trying to understand Johanna as a person, he sees her in terms of mythological figures—usually ambiguous ones. Perhaps he found her attractive—all these women were attractive. Beethoven seems to have distrusted the effects of sexual attraction—Circe's charms turned men into beasts.

The Queen of the Night in Mozart's *The Magic Flute* is particularly ambiguous: she implores the hero to free her daughter from captivity and the audience sympathizes. Then the audience's view of the situation is reversed: Sarastro, the daughter's captor-guardian, is revealed as a sage, preparing the hero and the daughter for marriage when they have reached a higher stage of enlightenment. The Queen of the Night now seems to be evil, threatening this sage. But her mother-love still seems genuine. Perhaps she is not wise enough to see what is really for her child's good?

Perhaps Beethoven saw himself in the role of the sage Sarastro, knowing what was best for Karl and his mother. Sometimes he shows genuine sympathy for Johanna, understanding how she felt at being kept away from her son, or fearing that a particular restriction on her might humiliate her. In 1824, when she was ill, he aided her financially.

But he wanted to separate her from Karl, on whom he felt she was a bad influence. He wanted the boy to be all his—a family of his own—and he resented other claims on Karl. He sometimes signed his letters to Karl, "your true father," as if wishing it could make it so. He genuinely loved the boy, and worried continually about him—too much so for the boy's good or comfort. He prayed with Karl morning and night, and got Carl Czerny to teach him music, hoping to make him a musician. He put Karl in a good boarding school, then took him out and hired a private tutor, then decided a good public school was best, then put him back into the boarding school. When a court intervened, Karl was put into another school.

These constant changes must have left Karl uncertain that anything would last, an effect increased by Beethoven's tendency to treat him with alternate severity and indulgence. By the time he was fourteen, his school reports called him unsteady and lazy—it is easy to see why. Still, no doubt Uncle Ludwig's ways were not too different from those of Karl's father.

Hardest on Karl must have been the constant pressure to take sides between his mother and his uncle. Beethoven ordered Karl not to see his mother, and thought Johanna bribed his servants in order to see Karl secretly. If she did, one can hardly blame her. When Karl went to see her against his orders, Beethoven felt betrayed. Karl tried sometimes to please his uncle, sometimes his mother. He complained that his uncle often wouldn't believe him if he told the truth, and made him tell lies about what his mother said to him about his uncle. Beethoven occasionally shook or hit him, and tried to persuade him to hate his mother. He felt a strong need to believe her evil, and to have Karl believe her so: then he would not be to blame for separating mother and son, and Karl would belong only to him.

In 1818 Johanna sued to acquire the guardianship of Karl, feeling that he was not being raised well. During this period the boy ran away to his mother. Beethoven felt betrayed, and cried out tearfully to a friend, "He is ashamed of me." No doubt Karl must often have been embarrassed by his uncle. A child wants his parents to seem normal to the world; Karl had to walk down the streets of Vienna with an eccentric uncle—poorly dressed, not very clean, so deaf that he didn't know when he was making odd noises as he walked. Beethoven had always been somewhat paranoid: under the stress of worrying about Karl and his law cases, he became more so. There were rumors that he had become insane. He lacked control of his emotions, suspected people groundlessly, and believed himself impoverished, though he was not.

One evening Beethoven was arrested outside of Vienna because a policeman thought he looked like a tramp. When Beethoven told the policeman who he was, the man doubted his word, saying, "You're a tramp; Beethoven doesn't look that way." (The policeman at least knew Beethoven's name: is there any living composer now known to an average policeman?) Finally a friend came to identify Beethoven at eleven at night, and he was freed.

After Johanna sued to regain custody of Karl in 1818, Beethoven spent an enormous amount of time and energy preparing for trial. After another court rejected jurisdiction, the city court appointed a temporary guardian, then in spite of all Beethoven could do through the influence of his patrons, gave Johanna the guardianship in the fall of 1819. Beethoven's brother Johann became involved in the quarrel, siding with Johanna. In 1820 Beethoven took the case to the Appeals Court, using Archduke Rudolph's influence; Johanna hurt her own cause by giving birth to an illegitimate daughter—whom she named Ludovica, the female form of Ludwig! The Appeals Court gave custody back to Beethoven.

These five years of affection, pain, and anxiety affected Beethoven greatly. He composed much less than he had in the past. His health began to deteriorate: the first symptoms of jaundice appeared, an early indication of the cirrhosis which was to kill him. We may wish that Beethoven had never become involved with the care of Karl, and think he might have written many great works during the time he spent on Karl's affairs. But even a great artist is entitled to have an emotional life. His relationship to Karl, however much grief it caused him, gave Beethoven something that meant a great deal to him—a family of his own, someone to love, a connection tying him to the rest of the race despite his deafness.

Beethoven and the Police, Vienna, 1822

Many thanks to the Bundespolizeidirektion Wien for supplying us with the proper uniform.

Chapter Eleven

In the six years after 1815 Beethoven finished so few new works that a rumor spread that he couldn't compose any more. Karl's problems took time and thought that should have gone to composing, but this failure in creativity was only apparent. Beethoven was working on several massive pieces: works on the scale of the *Missa Solemnis* and the Ninth Symphony required years of thought while Beethoven struggled to understand what he wanted to achieve and how best to organize his material.

While Beethoven was working on the Ninth, a friend asked him to describe how he composed. "I carry my thoughts about with me for a long time, sometimes a very long time, before I set them down. At the same time my memory is so faithful to me that I am sure not to forget a theme which I have once conceived, even after years have passed. I make many changes, reject and reattempt until I am satisfied. Then the working-out in breadth, length, height and depth begins in my head, and since I am conscious of what I want, the basic idea never leaves me. It rises, grows upward, and I hear and see the picture as a whole take shape and stand before me as though cast in a single piece, so that all that is left is the work of writing it down. This goes quickly, according as I have the time, for sometimes I have several compositions in labor at once, though I am sure never to confuse one with the other. You will ask me whence I take my ideas? That I cannot say with any degree of certainty; they come to me uninvited, directly or indirectly. I could almost grasp them in my hands, out in Nature's open, in the woods, during my promenades, in the silence of the night, at the earliest dawn. They are roused by moods, which in the poet's case are transmuted into words, and in mine into tones, that sound, roar and storm until at last they take shape for me as notes." No wonder, however, with all the thought and revision, that Beethoven once said, "To begin a big work makes me shudder."

Mozart had been able to make composing look easy—which must have infuriated all his contemporaries, who had to work very hard to write music half as good as Mozart's. Beethoven never made composing look easy, nor was it easy for him. His sketchbooks sometimes allow us to look over his shoulder as he hammered his ideas out on the anvil until they became what he wanted. In the score of one of his late quartets he wrote on the margin, *"Muss es sein? Doch muss es sein!"* ["Must it be? It must be thus!"] Through determination and the power to keep working until he was satisfied Beethoven achieved the tremendous strength of his music. His pieces in their final form seem inevitable: it is impossible to conceive of a major Beethoven work being otherwise, it seems so right.

The composer pours a pitcher of water over his head while at work

But while Beethoven was struggling with several long works, his income suffered. As he could no longer make money by performing as a pianist or by conducting, his income came from his pension, gifts in response to dedications, the interest on the bank shares he had bought with his profits from the concerts in his year of great successes, and the sale of his works to publishers. Less money came from publishers now, and Beethoven had heavy expenses—Karl's care and schooling; lawyers; his summers in the country; and usually at least two servants, required by the needs of a boy and a man so deaf his friends had to write notes to communicate with him. Beethoven got into debt, and thought himself very poor. He refused to sell his bank shares, which he thought of as held in trust for Karl. He worried about providing for Karl, and for his own old age.

In fact Beethoven's income was probably large enough to meet his needs if he had known how to use it properly; but Beethoven never understood his own finances. He tried to help matters by getting as much as he could for his works from publishers, sometimes behaving unethically. He even sold the same work to different publishers, and when the Philharmonic Society of London paid him for three new overtures, he sold them three old ones instead, to their distress. The only excuse for his behavior is that he seems to have felt that a man who was creating great music deserved to be free of financial worries.

Those who understood music revered Beethoven and his works, and musical visitors to Vienna tried to meet Beethoven. He did not receive most visitors, objecting to being distracted, but those who did meet him were impressed. Gioacchino Rossini, the most popular opera composer of the age, called on Beethoven; years later he described to Richard Wagner how none of the Beethoven portraits captured "the indefinable sadness spread across all his features, so that from under heavy eyebrows there shone, as if from the depths of caverns, two eyes which, though small, seemed to pierce you." Beethoven, who managed to keep informed about the works of other composers, praised Rossini's comic operas, and Rossini left him sadly, feeling the contrast between his existence, feted at banquets by the nobility, and the squalor in which Beethoven lived.

Friedrich Rochlitz, a music critic who met Beethoven in 1822, listened as Beethoven spoke to his friends while dining at an inn. (They replied by writing notes in his conversation book.) "His remarks all were made with the greatest unconcern and without the least reserve, and whatever he said was spiced with highly original naïve judgements or humorous fancies. He impressed me as being a man with a rich aggressive intellect, an unlimited, never resting imagination..."

A deaf Beethoven using his conversation book

At a later meeting in Baden, Rochlitz talked with Beethoven. "During the entire visit he was uncommonly gay and at times most amusing and all that entered his mind had to come out. ('Well, it happens that I am unbuttoned today,' he said...) His talk and his actions all formed a chain of eccentricities, in part most peculiar. Yet they all radiated a truly childlike amiability, carelessness, and confidence in everyone who approached him. Even his barking tirades...are only explosions of his fanciful imagination and his momentary excitement. They are uttered without haughtiness, without any feeling of bitterness and hatefulness—and are simply blustered out lightly, good-humoredly, the offsprings of a mad, humorous mood. In his life he often shows—and for the sake of his own subsistence only too often and too decidedly—that to the very person who has grievously injured him, whom he has most violently denounced one moment, he will give his last dollar the next, should that person need it.

To this we must add the most cheerful recognition of merit in others, if only it be distinctive and individual. (How he speaks of Handel, Bach, Mozart!) He does not, however, where his greater works are concerned, allow others to find fault (and who would have the right to do so?) yet he never actually overvalues them: and with regard to his lesser things is more inclined, perhaps, to abandon them with a laugh than any other person. He does this the more since once he is in the vein, rough striking witticisms, droll conceits, surprising and exciting paradoxes suggest themselves to him in a continuous flow. Hence in all seriousness I claim that he even appears to be amiable. Or if you shrink from this word, I might say that the dark, unlicked bear seems so ingenuous and confiding, growls and shakes his shaggy pelt so harmlessly and grotesquely that it is a pleasure, and one has to be kind to him, even though he were nothing but a bear in fact and had done no more than a bear's best."

People often used the word "child-like" in describing Beethoven: like a child he voiced his emotions of the moment, but quickly forgot his hostilities. His basic good-heartedness, his talent, and his need kept his friends fond of him in spite of the worst things he said or did.

During these years several major pieces occupied Beethoven. When his faithful pupil and patron Archduke Rudolph was appointed Cardinal Archbishop of Olmutz in 1819, Beethoven decided to write a mass for the installation ceremonies in 1820. Afterthought followed afterthought, and the piece was not finished until 1823. Even then the score Beethoven sent Rudolph contains a few final changes. Beethoven's erasures in the tympani part of the *Agnus Dei* wore a hole in the very thick paper. No doubt Rudolph knew Beethoven well enough not to be surprised by the delays, and the *Missa Solemnis* was worth waiting for.

Another work of this period, the massive set of variations on a theme by Diabelli, also occupied him from 1819 to 1823 and also overran its original deadline. But the biggest and best-known work of this period was his Ninth Symphony. Many great men seem to have had in mind since early youth most of the projects they ultimately complete: Beethoven had first mentioned in 1793 his desire to compose a setting for Schiller's "Ode to Joy," the text for the final movement of this symphony. Since 1812 he had been working on ideas for a ninth and tenth symphony—often he seemed to work on two works of the same sort together: the Fifth and Sixth Symphonies, and the Seventh and Eighth, had been born as twins. In 1815 Beethoven came up with the theme of the scherzo; in 1817 he wrote extended sketches; in 1818 he thought of a choral movement as part of the symphony—something hitherto unheard of. By 1823 he finished his first movement, then worked on all the rest at once, finishing in February 1824.

Perhaps the subject of Schiller's ode—love and brotherhood—shamed Beethoven into repairing some of his family relationships. In 1822 he was reconciled with his brother Johann after ten years of alienation—ever since Beethoven had meddled with Johann's love life. The Beethoven brothers being what they were, they quarrelled again from time to time. Johann handled some of Beethoven's business affairs for him, often suggesting that his other friends were cheating him (Johann frequently suspected others of dishonesty, which suggests either that he shared Ludwig's paranoid tendency, or that his own business practices were shady); Ludwig often interfered in the problems of Johann's stormy marriage. Beethoven also reached a truce with Johanna when he offered financial aid during her illness in 1824.

After Beethoven finished the Ninth Symphony, he was not sure that the Viennese public would appreciate it. He thought of having it and the Mass performed in Berlin. Many of his friends felt that such a thing would shame their city; they organized the signing of a petition, which was presented to Beethoven, begging him to perform his work in Vienna. They were seconded by two pretty young singers, whose visits Beethoven always enjoyed. He was pleased, and agreed.

The concert on May 7, 1824 included the "Consecration of the House" Overture, three sections of the *Missa Solemnis* written for Rudolph (the censors made difficulties, on the grounds that religious music should not be performed in a theatre), and the Ninth Symphony. Karoline Unger and

58

Henriette Sontag, the two young singers who had become friends of Beethoven, were among the soloists. Some notes were too high for them, and they pled with Beethoven to change these; he refused. In performance the singers simply left out those notes they could not reach. Beethoven never knew. At the performance's end Karoline Unger plucked his sleeve to make him turn around, so that he could see the audience applauding, waving hats and handkerchiefs.

A tremendous reception of the Ninth Symphony, May 7, 1824

Chapter Twelve

Beethoven planned a fine dinner for the three friends who had helped him organize his successful concert. Just before it, he learned that his profit had been only about $900; brother Johann quickly suggested that someone had cheated him. At the dinner Beethoven ordered, then accused one friend of having helped cheat him; finally all three had to walk out, to have an unhappy dinner elsewhere.

More money came from a second performance, and the Philharmonic Society of London paid nearly as much again to perform the work. But they wanted Beethoven to come to London and write a new symphony for them. Beethoven wanted to go, but was nervous: a deaf man could not travel alone. Would the Philharmonic Society pay the expenses of a companion? Would he be comfortable in a strange country? Could he safely leave Karl?

Karl, now eighteen, was studying philology at the University of Vienna, and helping his uncle as a secretary. He wanted to become an independent adult, but Beethoven kept him under close restraint, giving him very little money and asking his friends to report on Karl's doings. Karl resented this, and asked to become an army officer: the army's discipline seemed freer and more dependable than his uncle's whims. Beethoven rejected the idea, but allowed Karl to transfer to the Polytechnic Institute, to study business.

Beethoven was often angry with Karl, and more often pained by his neglect. He complains in a letter that Karl had not let him know if he is well, or has done an errand for him. "The continual solitude weakens me even more, for often through my weakness I am really on the verge of feebleness. Oh do not pain me more; the man with the scythe will not be giving me much more time." (June 1825) Sometimes Beethoven reproaches the young man and threatens to cast him off entirely, sometimes he writes him tenderly:"My precious son! Go no further—come but to my arms, not a harsh word shall you hear. O God, do not rush away in your misery. You will be received as lovingly as ever. What to consider, what to do in the future, these things we will talk over affectionately. On my word of honor no reproaches, since they would in no case do good now. Henceforth you may expect from me only the most loving care and help—Do but come—Come to the faithful heart of

      your father Beethoven
Come home immediately upon receiving this.
[In French] If you do not you will surely kill me..."   (October 1825)

While the tension between Beethoven and Karl increased, Beethoven was working busily on what were to be his last major compositions. The Russian Prince Galitzin commissioned three string quartets in 1822. After thinking about the commission for some time, now Beethoven turned all his thoughts towards quartets. Eventually he wrote five of them, and an enormous final movement too large for the Opus 130 quartet for which it had been intended. This "Grosse Fugue" he published separately as Opus 133. (The other quartets are Opus 127, 131, 132, and 135.) While finishing these quartets Beethoven began early planning for a future Tenth Symphony—perhaps for London, a Requiem, oratorios like Handel's, and an overture on the theme B-A-C-H.

His new quartets baffled his contemporaries, and the next generation as well, but are now regarded as his bridge to the future, among his greatest works. They brought him little money, however, since Prince Galitzin developed financial problems, and never managed to pay for the works which make his name remembered. Beethoven's friends helped with his expenses at this time. When his clothes became too shabby, his friends took them away during the night, leaving new ones in their place. Beethoven never noticed—he put on whatever clothes were in front of him.

In October 1825 one of Beethoven's incessant moves brought him into the neighborhood where Stephan von Breuning lived. Beethoven had gotten angry at Stephan when he advised Beethoven not to take the guardianship of Karl, but was now happy to see him again, and their renewed friendship gave Beethoven great pleasure. The considerate von Breuning kept his wife from asking Beethoven to play the piano, because, "He doesn't like to do it, and I do not want to ask him because it might pain him not to hear himself."

Early in 1826 an illness kept Beethoven in bed for some time; increasingly his health was poor. In summer, as he was preparing for his usual move to the country, shocking news came.

He and Karl had been quarrelling. Beethoven thought Karl was not working hard enough, and was wasting his evenings in dissipation. Sometimes he would go to Karl's school, to escort him home for lunch like a small boy. Karl sometimes lied to his uncle, and referred to him as "the old fool." He got into debt, missed some exams, and talked about suicide. Beethoven's friends removed Karl's pistols. Karl pawned his watch and bought a new pair. On July 19 Karl tried to kill himself: he missed totally with the first pistol, then with the second put a bullet into his head—but he did not kill himself. He was carried to his mother's house to be nursed.

This blow shattered Beethoven. He must have asked himself what he had done wrong, and felt pain and guilt: how could someone he loved as much as

Karl hurt him so? He worried whether Karl's wound would heal without a fatal infection, and whether Karl would be arrested and tried: suicide was a crime in Austria. Beethoven's friends noticed that he looked much older.

The von Breunings had Beethoven eat with them so that he would not be alone. They felt Karl and Beethoven should be separated, so that Karl could escape the pressures he had felt. He had been torn between his mother and his uncle, driven by his uncle's demands that he meet standards beyond his powers, and frustrated by the lack of freedom to become himself; he said, "I grew worse because my uncle wanted me to be better." The von Breunings advised Beethoven to let Karl go into the army as he wished, and when Beethoven consented reluctantly, von Breuning got Karl a commission.

Meanwhile, a place was needed for Karl to stay until his wound healed and his regiment was ready to receive him. Johann van Beethoven offered the hospitality of his country house at Gneizendorf to Karl and Ludwig, who went there in late September. At first things went well: Beethoven and Karl played four-hand piano pieces together. But Beethoven was in poor health, and the cold weather made him worse. He was not an easy guest, sticking to his own habits. He got up at 5:30 and composed, sitting at a table, beating time with his hands and feet, and singing. After breakfasting with the family at 7:30 he would go for a walk in the fields, again composing—shouting and waving his arms, sometimes walking very rapidly, sometimes very slowly, pausing to make notes. One morning Beethoven met a peasant who was driving a pair of young oxen, not yet accustomed to the yoke. The oxen took fright at Beethoven, ran down a steep hill, and their driver found it hard to stop them and turn them around. Beethoven, who hadn't even noticed, came towards the peasant again, not hearing his shouts of anger, and stampeded the oxen once more. The peasant asked who that fool was: only the answer that he was the landlord's brother saved Beethoven from the peasant's rage.

Beethoven returned to the house for dinner at 12:30, went to his room till 3:00, then roamed the fields till nearly sunset. After supper at 7:30 he went to his room, wrote till 10:00, then went to bed.

Members of the Beethoven family never stayed together long without quarrelling. Ludwig and Karl still wrangled. Johann thought Karl should be off to the army, and Ludwig wanted to keep him. Ludwig still felt that Johann's wife was an immoral woman, and tried to bully his brother into making a will disinheriting her in favor of Karl. After one quarrel Ludwig refused to eat with the family any more, and took his meals in his own room. He asked a servant whom he trusted to report to him what other members of the family were saying about him.

His inspired singing causes an ox team to panic

Meanwhile his disease of the liver was making itself felt. Illness made his temper worse. After a final quarrel Ludwig insisted on leaving his brother's house and returning to Vienna. After travelling two days in an open carriage in December without winter clothing, he was ill when he reached Vienna, and had to call in the doctors.

The story of the last four months of Beethoven's life is mostly medical history. Briefly, he survived an attack of pneumonia, but developed dropsy as his liver failed. Four times the doctor cut into his swollen body to drain it of the fluid. Karl nursed him until his departure for the army January 2. Beethoven hoped to survive: he wrote his old Bonn friend Franz Wegeler, "I hope still to bring some great works into the world and then as an old child end my earthly course somewhere amongst good men." One great pleasure came during his illness—a gift. A visitor had heard Beethoven say, "Handel is the greatest composer who ever lived," and had resolved to send Beethoven the newly printed edition of Handel's works—all forty volumes! Beethoven propped the books against the wall by his bed to turn over the pages, and broke out from time to time in expressions of praise: "I can still learn from him."

Unable to work, Beethoven worried about money. He had his bank shares, but these were to be Karl's legacy, and he refused to sell them. Relief came from abroad: the directors of the London Philharmonic Society, hearing of his illness, sent him the noble gift of a hundred pounds—over a thousand dollars in today's values. He promised to send them his Tenth Symphony, on which he worked whenever he was allowed.

But it soon became clear, even to Beethoven, that he was not going to recover. He made his will, simply leaving everything to Karl; Stephan von Breuning would be Karl's guardian. He signed his will March 23, and several other documents. He was now so feeble that he omitted letters from his name in his trembling signature.

From the evening of the 24th until his death two days later he was unconscious or delirious. "His powerful frame, his unweakened lungs, fought like giants with approaching death. The spectacle was a fearful one," wrote Gerhard von Breuning, Stephan's son; the family were often with him, helping him.

After 5:00 in the afternoon of the 26th, there came a flash of lightning and a violent clap of thunder, unexpectedly lighting up the death chamber. "Beethoven opened his eyes, lifted his right hand and looked up for several seconds with his fist clenched and a very serious, threatening expression as if he wanted to say: 'Inimical powers, I defy you!' " With this gesture he died—apparently fighting to the end.

Chapter Thirteen

The next afternoon von Breuning, Johann van Beethoven, and other friends searched Beethoven's lodgings to find the bank shares he had left Karl. For some time no one could find them—Johann, always irritating, suggested that someone had stolen them. At last someone pulled out a nail protruding from a cabinet, and a concealed drawer fell out: in it were the bank shares, two portraits of women, Beethoven's copy of his love letter of 1812, and his copy of the Heiligenstadt Testament of 1805—a summary of his emotional life.

The funeral took place the afternoon of March 19th. Schools closed. Between fifteen and twenty thousand Viennese came to honor Beethoven. The funeral procession needed an hour and a half to get through the one block of jammed street between Beethoven's lodgings and the overflowing church. Singers carried his coffin, and friends and distinguished men carried torches—Czerny, the poet Grillparzer, young Franz Schubert. Johann van Beethoven and the von Breunings followed the coffin. (Karl arrived from the army too late for the funeral.) After Grillparzer's eulogy at the graveside the coffin was lowered into the grave, three laurel wreaths crowned it, and as earth was thrown on the coffin, the torches were extinguished.

Why did so many people turn out to honor Beethoven? Surely not all of them were music lovers capable of appreciating his works. Yet somehow they knew that he was a great man, and desired to be associated with greatness for once in their lives. From his earliest years people had seen Beethoven's great gift. But many people who start life with great talents do little with them. Family responsibilities, illness, the death of loved ones, unhappy loves, failures, and the daily distraction of life eat their time and energy. Beethoven survived these things and continued to create. He did not just survive; he overcame. "I will seize life by the throat and make it yield..." he once said.

Grillparzer in his eulogy said, "he was an artist, and all that was his, was his through art alone...He who comes after him will not continue him; he must begin anew, for he who went before left off only where art leaves off." Beethoven had hoped that his sacrifices of his private life for his art would be proved worthwhile by the value of the works he created. In 1803 he wrote a painter friend, "Continue to paint—and I shall continue to write down notes; and thus we shall live—for ever?—yes, perhaps, for ever." In his notebook he wrote, "What more can be given to man than fame and praise and immortality?" He questioned; perhaps he was never sure whether the cost was too great; but he achieved what he sought.